# ALZHEIMER'S DISEASE
## A DIFFICULT DIAGNOSIS

By Jennifer Lombardo

Portions of this book originally appeared in *Alzheimer's Disease* by Jacqueline Adams.

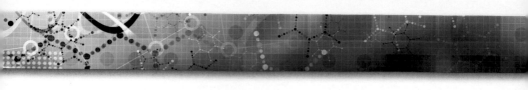

Published in 2018 by
**Lucent Press, an Imprint of Greenhaven Publishing LLC**
353 3rd Avenue
Suite 255
New York, NY 10010

Designer: Deanna Paternostro
Editor: Jennifer Lombardo

**Library of Congress Cataloging-in-Publication Data**

Names: Lombardo, Jennifer, author.
Title: Alzheimer's disease : a difficult diagnosis / Jennifer Lombardo.
Description: New York : Lucent Press, [2018] | Series: Diseases and disorders
    | Includes bibliographical references and index.
Identifiers: LCCN 2017043598| ISBN 9781534562820 (pbk. book) | ISBN
    9781534561892 (library bound book) | ISBN 9781534561885 (ebook)
Subjects: LCSH: Alzheimer's disease–Diagnosis. | Alzheimer's
    disease–Treatment.
Classification: LCC RC523 .L66 2018 | DDC 616.8/311–dc23
LC record available at https://lccn.loc.gov/2017043598

Printed in the United States of America

CPSIA compliance information: Batch #CW18KL: For further information contact Greenhaven Publishing LLC, New York, New York at 1-844-317-7404.

Please visit our website, www.greenhavenpublishing.com. For a free color catalog of all our high-quality books, call toll free 1-844-317-7404 or fax 1-844-317-7405.

# CONTENTS

Illness is an unfortunate part of life, and it is one that is often misunderstood. Thanks to advances in science and technology, people have been aware for many years that diseases such as the flu, pneumonia, and chicken pox are caused by viruses and bacteria. These diseases all cause physical symptoms that people can see and understand, and many people have dealt with these diseases themselves. However, sometimes diseases that were previously unknown in most of the world turn into epidemics and spread across the globe. Without an awareness of the method by which these diseases are spread—through the air, through human waste or fluids, through sexual contact, or by some other method—people cannot take the proper precautions to prevent further contamination. Panic often accompanies epidemics as a result of this lack of knowledge.

Knowledge is power in the case of mental disorders, as well. Mental disorders are just as common as physical disorders, but due to a lack of awareness among the general public, they are often stigmatized. Scientists have studied them for years and have found that they are generally caused by hormonal imbalances in the brain, but they have not yet determined with certainty what causes those imbalances or how to fix them. Because even mild mental illness is stigmatized in Western society, many people prefer not to talk about it.

Chronic pain disorders are also not well understood—even by researchers—and do not yet have foolproof treatments. People who have a mental disorder or a disease or disorder that causes them to feel chronic pain can be the target of uninformed opinions. People who do not have these disorders sometimes struggle to understand how difficult it can be to deal with the symptoms. These disorders are often termed "invisible illnesses" because no one can see the symptoms; this leads many people to doubt that they exist or are serious problems. Additionally, people who have an undiagnosed disorder may understand that they are experiencing the world in a different way than their peers, but they have no one to turn to for answers.

Misinformation about all kinds of ailments is often spread through personal anecdotes, social media, and even news sources. This series aims to present accurate information about both physical and mental conditions so young adults will have a better understanding of them. Each volume discusses the symptoms of a particular disease or disorder, ways it is currently being treated, and the research that is being done to understand it further. Advice for people who may be suffering from a disorder is included, as well as information for their loved ones about how best to support them.

With fully cited quotes, a list of recommended books and websites for further research, and informational charts, this series provides young adults with a factual introduction to common illnesses. By learning more about these ailments, they will be better able to prevent the spread of contagious diseases, show compassion to people who are dealing with invisible illnesses, and take charge of their own health.

# UNDERSTANDING ALZHEIMER'S

Most people have heard of Alzheimer's disease—often called Alzheimer's or AD—but not everyone understands how it affects its victims and their loved ones. There are many myths surrounding the disease, and the way it is shown on TV and in the movies is not always accurate. Many people believe Alzheimer's only affects elderly people or that it simply makes people forgetful. The reality is that Alzheimer's is a deadly disease with no currently known cure, and its symptoms can cause a lot of distress for patients and their friends and families.

When John's father began showing symptoms of memory loss, his family thought it was simply forgetfulness that goes along with normal aging. As the symptoms worsened, they realized the situation was more serious. At age 80, he was diagnosed with Alzheimer's.

John's father and other family members were ready to seek help when they became aware of the problem, but that is not always the case. Alzheimer's is such a dreaded disease that sufferers often try to hide their symptoms out of embarrassment or fear of a diagnosis that will confirm the worst. Family members or victims of the disease may be in denial, refusing to admit that something is wrong. At times, one close family member may battle to convince others that a problem exists and that their loved one needs to see a doctor. Because people with Alzheimer's may forget things one day and remember them the next, others sometimes mistakenly believe they are faking the memory loss.

For many years, people thought the symptoms of Alzheimer's were a normal part of aging. Despite scientific breakthroughs in the past several decades, myths about Alzheimer's persist. For instance, some people believe all elderly people with memory problems have Alzheimer's or that the disease affects only older people. Although Alzheimer's is the most common cause of memory loss in the elderly, many other causes exist, and although the risk for Alzheimer's does increase with age, it can strike people in their 30s, 40s, or 50s.

It is a myth that extreme forgetfulness is a normal part of aging. Many elderly people without dementia remain independent and active.

Other myths are that a diagnosis of Alzheimer's means that a person's life is over and that people with Alzheimer's are not aware of what goes on around them. Many people with Alzheimer's live meaningful lives, using their time in the early stages of the disease to care for matters that are important to them. The effects of the disease on a person's cognitive, or thinking, abilities vary with the individual and with time, but people with Alzheimer's may still understand what is happening, and they appreciate being treated with respect.

Knowledge about Alzheimer's helps family members not only show respect but also deal with their own pain. When his father fails to recognize him, John reminds himself that the disease is to blame. The children in the family are aware of the problem and do their best to interact with their grandfather. John said, "We just can talk to him the way we always talked to him. We might not get the same answer, or what we expect."[1]

With their ongoing search for knowledge about Alzheimer's, scientists hope to do more than dispel myths and misunderstandings. Many studies arc targeting ways to identify people who are at risk for the disease and to diagnose sufferers earlier. Researchers are working to gain insight into the causes of Alzheimer's. They hope this will allow them to develop effective ways not only to treat Alzheimer's but also to prevent it from developing at all.

## CHAPTER ONE

# MORE THAN FORGETFULNESS

The most well-known symptom of Alzheimer's is memory loss, but there are other symptoms of the disease. These include irritability, aggression, personality changes, depression, loss of appetite, lack of self-control, and paranoia. These symptoms make the disease difficult for the victim to handle; they may not always understand that their emotional reactions to things are sometimes inappropriate. Alzheimer's is also stressful for the caretakers of the sufferer. It is upsetting for them to watch someone they love slowly turn into a different person. However, with support from others who know what they are going through, the friends and family of a patient with Alzheimer's will have a much easier time dealing with the challenges they face.

## A Difficult Disease

As people age, they often become somewhat forgetful but can still function normally in their daily lives. They may take longer to remember something, or they may rely more on calendars or notes. However, they can still handle daily tasks, and they do not behave in inappropriate ways.

With Alzheimer's, the situation is different. The symptoms go far beyond the forgetfulness that often goes along with aging. Memory loss becomes so severe that it interferes with daily living. Other cognitive abilities, such as use of language, math, and the ability to recognize familiar objects and people, are gradually lost. Alzheimer's also alters a person's behavior and ability to perform everyday tasks. "Alzheimer's Disease is a condition that affects the whole way someone is," said James Galvin, a neurology, psychiatry, and population health professor at New York University's Langone Medical Center. "It affects their personality. It affects their behavior. It affects their thinking. It affects their memory. It affects their ability to speak."[2]

Even though aging itself does not explain Alzheimer's, the risk of developing Alzheimer's does increase with age. Most cases of Alzheimer's occur in people 65 years of age or older. This is sometimes called late-onset Alzheimer's. After age 65, the number of people with Alzheimer's doubles with every 5-year increase in age. Only 5 percent of patients with Alzheimer's have early-onset Alzheimer's, which can strike people as early as their 30s, but it is more often seen after age 40.

Early-onset Alzheimer's can strike people as young as 30, but this is very rare.

People often confuse Alzheimer's with other types of dementia—conditions in which the brain's ability to function is affected to the point that it interferes with daily life. Doctors have found over 100 different causes of dementia, including other neurodegenerative diseases, infections, and vitamin deficiencies. Alzheimer's is the most common cause of dementia in the United States, responsible for 60 to 80 percent of cases. Some forms of dementia are reversible, but

Alzheimer's is not one of them. Researchers believe the damage begins decades before symptoms appear.

## What Are the Signs of Alzheimer's?

- forgetting recent events and conversations, important dates, and facts recently learned

- repeating or asking the same question over and over

- getting lost; not knowing location and time

- problems with language, such as using the wrong words for items or stopping in the middle of a sentence and being unable to finish

- trouble with familiar tasks, such as driving or cooking

- problems with tasks requiring planning and organization, such as paying bills, making a grocery list, or following a recipe

- trouble with tasks involving math or numbers

- losing items because of an inability to remember where items were placed or last used

- difficulty judging distances

- poor judgment, such as giving too much money to telemarketers, going alone into dangerous areas, or failing to attend to personal hygiene

- personality changes, such as becoming depressed, confused, impulsive, suspicious, or easily angered

- withdrawal from social activities; loss of interest in activities once enjoyed

## Changes Over Time

Once symptoms become noticeable, Alzheimer's progresses in three stages: mild, or early-stage; moderate, or middle-stage; and severe, or late-stage. In the early stage, people have trouble remembering what happened recently, although older memories remain. They may forget the names of people they have just been introduced to or have problems thinking of the right word in a conversation. Other problems arise, such as getting lost and taking longer to complete everyday activities. Sufferers also begin to slowly lose the ability to handle tasks that take planning and organization, such as making a grocery list or balancing a checkbook. Small mood and personality changes may appear.

In the middle stage, which lasts the longest of the three stages, the earlier problems continue to worsen and new problems appear. Sufferers may no longer be able to recognize people they know or be aware of where they are or what the date is. They stop being able to learn new things, and activities with multiple steps, such as dressing, become difficult. Not everyone with Alzheimer's experiences behavioral problems, but some common problems in this stage are wandering, restlessness, sleep trouble, and personality changes. A formerly mild person may become aggressive and threaten, hit, or accuse others. A formerly energetic person may seem uninterested and depressed. Impulsive behavior, delusions, and paranoia often arise. For instance, a person may believe that family members have stolen items he or she has misplaced. Throughout this stage, the person needs an increased level of care.

In the mild and moderate stages, symptoms can come and go. A person often seems to improve and remember things one day and then forget them the next. Because of this, misunderstandings sometimes

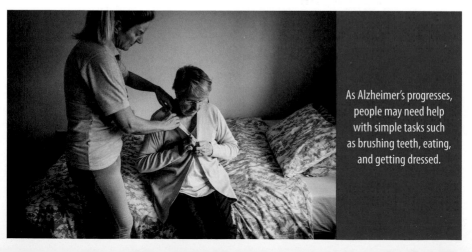

As Alzheimer's progresses, people may need help with simple tasks such as brushing teeth, eating, and getting dressed.

arise. Family and friends may become frustrated and wonder if the person is faking the memory problems.

By the time the disease has progressed to the late stage, the brain is damaged to the point that the person needs help to accomplish even the most basic tasks, such as sitting up or walking. Sufferers no longer remember family members or even themselves. They lose control of bladder and bowels and may remain in bed most of the time. Some also lose the ability to speak and can make only grunting or moaning noises. Because they have trouble swallowing, they may stop eating. They remain completely dependent on others until the disease results in their death. This final stage generally lasts from one to three years. Depending on factors such as the person's age and physical health, it may extend longer. Most patients with Alzheimer's live for an average of four to eight years after the disease is diagnosed, but some live twenty years or more, depending on individual factors.

## Not a Recent Development

Although Alzheimer's has become well-known as the cause of such devastating symptoms only in recent decades, ancient writers also described mental conditions that struck later in life. Most of them believed the loss of mental abilities was a natural part of aging.

More than 2,500 years ago, the Greek philosopher and mathematician Pythagoras stated that in old age, a person's mental abilities decline to the point that they act like children again. Two centuries later, the Greek philosopher Aristotle wrote that in the elderly, "there is not much left of the acumen of the mind which helped them in their youth, nor of the faculties which served the intellect, and which some call judgment, imagination, power of reasoning and memory."[3]

On the other hand, the Roman philosopher Cicero of the second century BC argued that the loss of mental abilities does not always accompany old age. He believed people could prevent mental decline by keeping their minds active and stated that "it is our duty to resist old age; to compensate for its defects by a watchful care; to fight against it as we would fight against disease."[4]

In the second century AD, the Roman doctor Galen listed old age as one of the causes of a condition he called *morosis*. He described patients with this problem as "some in whom the knowledge of letters and other arts are totally obliterated; indeed they can't even remember their own names."[5]

Near the end of the 18th century, Scottish physician William Cullen classified loss of mental abilities in the elderly as a medical condition called "amentia senilis." He defined it as "imbecility of judgement, by which men either do not perceive the relation of things or forget them due to diminished perception and memory when oppressed with age."[6] Doctors later used the term "senile dementia" to refer to this condition. Today, doctors do not use the word "senile," as it has taken on a negative meaning when it is used in conversation. When people say a person is "going senile," they are rudely implying that the person they are talking about is losing their cognitive functioning. This term should never be used to refer to someone with Alzheimer's or another type of dementia.

The ancient Greeks and Romans knew about Alzheimer's, although they did not call it that. Some, such as Pythagoras, thought it was a normal part of aging. Others, such as Cicero, believed it could be prevented.

## Dr. Alzheimer's Patient

Because doctors associated dementia with old age, a case that arose near the turn of the 20th century puzzled them. In 1901, German neurologist and psychiatrist Alois Alzheimer began treating a woman with severe dementia symptoms. He referred to her in his notes as Auguste D. Because she was only 51 years old—much younger than most patients with dementia—doctors believed her illness must have a different cause. In his notes, Alzheimer described his work with the patient:

> *When she has to write Mrs Auguste D., she writes Mrs and we must repeat the other words because she forgets them. The patient is not able to progress in writing and repeats, "I have lost myself."*

> *Reading, she passes from one line to the other and repeats the same line three times. But she correctly reads the letters. She seems not to understand what she reads. She accents the words in an unusual way. Suddenly she says, "Twins." "I know Mr. Twin." She repeats the word* twin *during the whole interview.*[7]

Her symptoms also included hallucinations and unpredictable behavior. Alzheimer wrote,

> *During the physical examination she cooperates and does not show anxiety. She suddenly says, "Just now a child called. Is he there?" She hears him calling … When she was brought from the isolation room to the bed she became agitated, screamed, and was noncooperative. She shows great fear and repeats, "I will not be cut." "I do not cut myself."*[8]

Auguste D.'s condition worsened over the following years. Before she died in 1906, she was completely bedridden, unable to speak, and dependent on the hospital's staff to feed her and keep her clean.

## Examining the Brain

After Auguste D.'s death, Alzheimer examined her

brain tissue to try to learn the cause of her illness. He observed atrophy, or shrinkage, of her brain, which resulted from the death of many neurons—cells that send messages from the brain to the other parts of the body. Other doctors had already observed brain atrophy in patients with dementia. When Alzheimer prepared slides of Auguste D.'s brain tissue with a new type of stain that allowed him to see the parts of neurons beneath a microscope, he discovered two abnormal features that surprised him.

The first surprise was that threadlike parts of neurons known as fibrils had tangled together into bundles. As these abnormal structures, which doctors now call neurofibrillary tangles, had grown, the neurons had disintegrated and died. The other abnormal structures were plaques—clumps of a sticky substance, later identified as amyloid protein—that had built up between neurons. Together, neurofibrillary tangles and amyloid plaques were the hallmarks of what Alzheimer believed to be a newly identified disease.

Amyloid plaques, shown here, are one telltale feature of Alzheimer's disease.

Doctors went on to identify other cases of people younger than 65 with the same symptoms and brain damage. In 1910, when psychiatrist Emil Kraepelin wrote a new edition of his *Textbook of Psychiatry*, he named the illness Alzheimer's disease. He wrote, "The clinical significance of this Alzheimer's Disease is still at the present time unclear. Although the anatomic findings would suggest the assumption that this is a matter of a particularly severe form of senile dementia, to some extent this is contradicted by the circumstance that the illness at times already begins at the end of the 40th year."[9] In other words, even though the symptoms looked like those of dementia, doctors thought the patients were too young. They considered Alzheimer's to be a separate condition, which they called pre-senile dementia.

In the following years, doctors examined brain tissue from hundreds of deceased patients who had suffered from similar symptoms. They found the same tangles and plaques in the brains of older people with dementia as they found in younger people who had been diagnosed with pre-senile dementia, or Alzheimer's. Still, most doctors believed dementia resulted from normal aging, so they thought younger patients must have a separate disease.

## Research Leads to Understanding

The confusion continued for decades, with older patients being diagnosed with senile dementia and younger patients with the same symptoms being diagnosed with pre-senile dementia, or Alzheimer's. Because cases of younger sufferers were less common, Alzheimer's was considered a rare disease.

Doctors sometimes debated whether or not dementia and Alzheimer's were the same disease, but very little research was performed. In the 1950s and 1960s, researchers used new technology—electron microscopes—to examine plaques and tangles. The differences they found between the brains of older people with and without dementia provided evidence that dementia does not result from normal aging. Rather, people with dementia were victims of a disease—the same disease that sometimes struck younger people. Researchers came to realize that no matter how old or young the patients were, they all suffered from Alzheimer's, which was not a rare disease after all.

Most people were unaware of the results of this research. Very little funding was set aside for studying Alzheimer's, and the disease received little public attention. That began to change in 1976, when neurologist Robert Katzman wrote an editorial in the *Archives of Neurology*. From his research, Katzman realized that not only were Alzheimer's and dementia the same illness but also that many people with Alzheimer's had been misdiagnosed with other types of dementia. He estimated that Alzheimer's was the fourth or fifth leading cause of death in the United States. He added,

> *The argument that Alzheimer disease is a major killer rests on the assumption that Alzheimer disease and senile dementia are a single process and should, therefore, be considered a single disease. Both Alzheimer disease and senile dementia are progressive dementias with similar changes in mental and neurological status that are indistinguishable by careful clinical analyses.*[10]

As awareness about Alzheimer's grew, so did funding for research. In the early 1980s, Katzman helped found the organization that later became known as the Alzheimer's Association, which provides private funding for research, support for people with Alzheimer's and their families, and public education about the disease. In the United States, Congress began setting aside more funds for Alzheimer's research through the National Institute on Aging (NIA). T. Franklin Williams, who served as the director of the NIA from 1983 to 1991, stated that "we had come to recognize that Alzheimer's dementia was probably the greatest scourge and disaster for older people and their families in the United States, and as well the growing potential in our scientific community to address its challenges. We made Alzheimer's research our highest priority."[11]

During this time, researchers gained insight into the formation of amyloid plaques and neurofibrillary tangles and developed new techniques for studying Alzheimer's. In 1998, neurologist François Boller and speech and language pathologist Margaret M. Forbes wrote in a medical article, "This improved understanding has led to a completely new attitude toward dementia which is no longer considered an unavoidable part of aging. Alzheimer's disease has become a 'household' word and it is not unusual to hear families of AD subjects as well as patients with diagnosis of AD discuss freely the condition with relatives or even with strangers."[12]

## Celebrities with Alzheimer's

For many diseases, a celebrity's discussion of their own personal battle can raise awareness and decrease stigma. For instance, Kristen Bell—the voice of Princess Anna in *Frozen*—has spoken out about her experience with anxiety and depression, and author John Green has written about his obsessive compulsive disorder (OCD). However, since Alzheimer's mainly affects people who are older than 60, celebrities who have it may no longer be familiar to young adults. Some of these include musicians John Mann and Malcolm Young, both of whom have recently begun speaking out about their experiences with Alzheimer's.

Rosa Parks, one of the heroes of the civil rights movement, developed Alzheimer's later in life.

Some people who are widely famous have already died from the disease without publicly announcing that they had it. These include Rosa Parks; E.B. White, the author of *Charlotte's Web*; and actor Gene Wilder, who starred in the 1971 movie *Willy Wonka and the Chocolate Factory*.

## How Much of a Problem Is Alzheimer's?

According to reports by the Alzheimer's Association, Alzheimer's is on the rise. It was the seventh leading cause of death in the United States in 2010, and every 70 seconds, someone developed the disease. By 2017, it was the sixth leading cause of death, with someone developing it every 66 seconds. More than 5 million Americans have Alzheimer's, but experts believe this number could rise to as much as 16 million by 2050. Race and sex appear to play a role in disease development; women are more likely to have it than men, and African Americans and Latinx are more likely to have it than older whites. The exact reasons for these differences are still unknown, but many researchers believe it has to do with genetics.

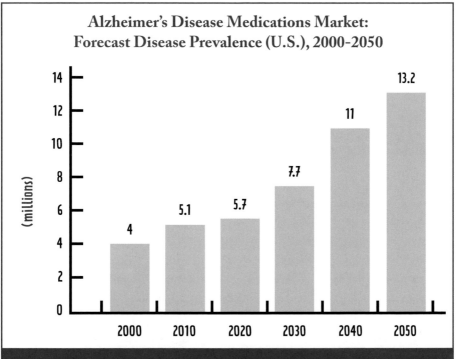

**Alzheimer's Disease Medications Market: Forecast Disease Prevalence (U.S.), 2000-2050**

This information from Health Wire shows the forecasted number of people who will develop Alzheimer's disease in the United States by 2050.

Besides patients with Alzheimer's, millions of other people are affected by the disease. The Alzheimer's Association reported that in 2016, an estimated 15.9 million people served as unpaid caregivers for someone with Alzheimer's or another dementia. The majority of the caregivers were family members, and the rest were friends. Each caregiver spent an average of 21.9 hours per week tending to the needs of a patient with dementia. This added up to 12.5 billion hours of unpaid caregiving in a single year. Additionally, there is a gender gap in terms of caregiving. In 2014, a study conducted by researchers at Princeton University in New Jersey found that women are much more likely to be caregivers than men. This may be because society trains women to believe they must be nurturing while training men to believe they should avoid this type of "women's work." The Princeton study and others have shown that if a woman steps into a caregiver role, a man is more likely to let her do more than her fair share of work and that women are more likely to allow this to happen because they are afraid the necessary work will not get done if they do not do it.

The disease also takes an economic toll. The costs of health care and long-term care for people with Alzheimer's and other dementias were expected to total $259 billion in 2017. No figures exist to measure the emotional and mental costs for patients with Alzheimer's and their loved ones.

Despite growing awareness of the problem and its scope, most sufferers do not receive a diagnosis until the disease is already in the moderate stage. Accurate methods of diagnosis are available, and early diagnosis carries many benefits for patients and their families.

## CHAPTER TWO

# ALZHEIMER'S AND OTHER DEMENTIAS

Although Alzheimer's is the most common cause of dementia, there are many other types of dementia. It can be difficult for doctors to tell them apart, especially in the early stages. Even after a diagnosis is made, there is still a small chance it will be wrong, since an autopsy is the only way to tell for sure whether a person has the plaques and tangles associated with Alzheimer's.

As with other debilitating diseases, such as cancer and diabetes, early diagnosis is key for successful treatment. However, many people are not diagnosed with Alzheimer's until the disease has progressed past the beginning stages. This may be because they are afraid to hear bad news or because they falsely believe their memory lapses are just part of getting older. "Usually, the early signs and symptoms are interpreted as normal aging,"[13] said neurologist Oscar Lopez, director of the University of Pittsburgh Alzheimer Disease Research Center (ADRC). Only later, when the symptoms become worse, do they realize a problem exists.

## Neurodegenerative Causes of Dementia

A dementia evaluation allows doctors to determine the cause of the problem so they can prescribe appropriate treatment. Because many other conditions have similar symptoms, these must be ruled out for a person to be diagnosed with Alzheimer's. Some of the other conditions that cause dementia are also neurodegenerative diseases, which destroy brain cells over time.

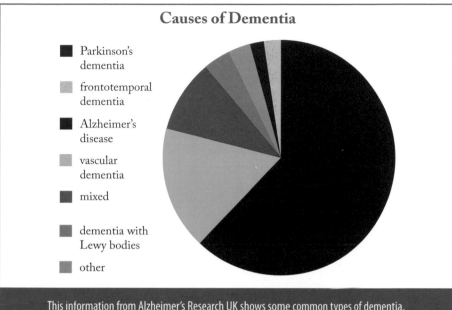

**Causes of Dementia**

- Parkinson's dementia
- frontotemporal dementia
- Alzheimer's disease
- vascular dementia
- mixed
- dementia with Lewy bodies
- other

This information from Alzheimer's Research UK shows some common types of dementia.

The second most common cause of dementia is vascular dementia, a neurodegenerative disease caused by decreased blood flow to the brain. This can happen when a blood vessel that brings oxygen to the brain either bursts or is blocked by a blood clot, resulting in a stroke. High blood pressure, atherosclerosis (hardening and narrowing of arteries), or other conditions that affect blood flow may also cause vascular dementia. The symptoms generally begin suddenly and worsen quickly, unlike the gradual onset and worsening of Alzheimer's symptoms. Patients with vascular dementia lose planning and organizational skills and have trouble with language and balance, but their memory problems may not be as severe as those of people with Alzheimer's.

Abnormal protein deposits called Lewy bodies form inside neurons as part of another disease, known as dementia with Lewy bodies (DLB). People with this disease suffer from muscle stiffness, which causes a shuffling walk and stiff facial expression. Other symptoms include hallucinations, tremors, loss of coordination and thinking abilities, and memory problems.

People with Parkinson's disease also suffer from muscle stiffness and tremors caused by damage to the brain, but not all develop problems with thinking and memory. About 20 to 40 percent of patients with Parkinson's disease do go on to develop Parkinson's disease dementia. Lewy bodies also play a role in this disease.

Because Lewy bodies are involved in Alzheimer's, DLB, and Parkinson's disease dementia, the symptoms are similar and it can be difficult to tell one from the other, especially in the early stages. The Alzheimer's Association explained the differences between the three diseases:

> *The diagnosis is DLB when:*
> * *Dementia symptoms consistent with DLB develop first*
> * *When both dementia symptoms and movement symptoms are present at the time of diagnosis*
> * *When dementia symptoms appear within one year after movement symptoms.*
>
> *The diagnosis is Parkinson's disease dementia when a person is originally diagnosed with Parkinson's based on movement symptoms, and dementia symptoms don't appear until a year or more later …*
>
> *Key differences between Alzheimer's and DLB:*
> * *Memory loss tends to be a more prominent symptom in early Alzheimer's than in early DLB, although advanced DLB may cause memory problems in addition to its more typical effects on judgment, planning, and visual perception.*

- *Movement symptoms are more likely to be an important cause of disability early in DLB than in Alzheimer's, although Alzheimer's can cause problems with walking, balance, and getting around as it progresses to moderate and severe stages.*

- *Hallucinations, delusions, and misidentification of familiar people are significantly more frequent in early-stage DLB than in Alzheimer's.*

- *REM sleep disorder [acting out dreams] is more common in early DLB than in Alzheimer's.*

- *Disruption of the autonomic nervous system, causing a blood pressure drop on standing, dizziness, falls, and urinary incontinence, is much more common in early DLB than in Alzheimer's.*[14]

Other abnormal structures called Pick bodies form inside neurons when a person has Pick's disease, which is a type of disorder known as frontotemporal dementia (FTD). Pick bodies are clumps of tau proteins. In a healthy brain, tau proteins play a role in distributing nutrients throughout the brain; Pick bodies stop those nutrients from getting where they need to go, which causes irreversible brain damage. Other types of FTD include behavior variant frontotemporal dementia (bvFTD), which causes personality changes, and primary progressive aphasia (PPA), which causes changes in a person's ability to either speak or understand language. Unlike Alzheimer's, in which damage begins in brain areas involved with recent memory, damage in these diseases begins in the brain's frontal lobes. Symptoms often appear at an earlier age than in people with Alzheimer's, and thinking and behavior are affected before memory is. Problems with language—finding the right words, understanding the meaning of words, and repeating phrases over and over—get progressively worse. People with FTD may lose inhibitions and begin to act in ways that they normally would not. For example, they may begin swearing, shoplifting, or undressing in public.

# Treatable Causes of Dementia

Besides neurodegenerative diseases, many other conditions cause dementia. Wernicke-Korsakoff syndrome (WKS) results from a vitamin B1 (thiamine) deficiency. Since heavy drinking affects the body's ability to absorb vitamin B1, the most common cause of this syndrome is years of alcoholism. Other causes include malnourishment, eating disorders, and kidney dialysis. Early on, problems with learning and memory may be even worse than with Alzheimer's. Doctors treat the condition with vitamin B1 shots. When alcoholism is the cause, the dementia symptoms stop worsening or even improve if the person stops drinking early enough, but they may be irreversible if the problem continues longer.

Heavy drinking can interfere with the body's absorption of vitamin B1, which may cause dementia.

Less common causes of dementia include other vitamin deficiencies, infections such as HIV and syphilis, and disorders of the thyroid, kidneys, or liver. When spinal fluid is blocked from flowing through the brain and spinal cord, it builds up in the brain in a condition known as normal pressure hydrocephalus. This causes dementia, changes in speech and the way a person walks, and incontinence of bladder and bowels. Damage stops if the condition is treated early on by inserting a shunt that allows spinal fluid to drain from the brain.

Many medications or combinations of medications

can cause dementia symptoms, especially in people older than age 65. The effects are generally reversed when the medication is stopped, but one class of medication, called anticholinergic drugs, is linked to a risk of long-term dementia. These drugs include common over-the-counter medications such as Benadryl and Dimetapp. A 2016 study found that regular use of medications such as these may cause changes in the brain, especially in the hippocampus, an area associated with memory.

## Testing for Dementia

Doctors often give patients a screening test to detect memory and thinking problems. One of the most common is the Mini-Mental State Examination (MMSE). In this short test, the doctor asks a patient simple questions such as the year and the state and town they are currently in. The patient is also asked to complete several tasks, such as counting backward by sevens from 100, naming two objects the doctor holds up, making up and writing a sentence, and copying a drawing of different shapes.

Another common test is clock drawing. The patient is instructed to draw a clock face and put numbers on it. Then the doctor asks the patient to make the clock read a certain time, such as 10 minutes past 11. The MMSE is a useful tool to help doctors assess whether or not a person is showing signs of dementia, especially for those who have progressed past the earliest stages.

## Diagnosing Alzheimer's

Because symptoms of Alzheimer's and other dementias can seem similar, especially in the early stages, seeking a diagnosis from a doctor who is experienced with Alzheimer's is important. In some cases, a primary care physician (PCP) diagnoses the patient and prescribes treatment. Because PCPs have to have a general knowledge about many different health problems that could affect their patients, not all of them are familiar with specialized information on Alzheimer's. Patients are often referred to specialists such as neurologists, geriatricians, and psychiatrists for diagnosis. Clinics and research centers that specialize in dementia can provide a thorough evaluation.

There is no single test for Alzheimer's; doctors look at multiple factors, including a patient's medical history, test results for mental and emotional status, and physical test results such as blood tests and brain scans. In order to receive an Alzheimer's diagnosis, the problems a person is experiencing must involve a significant loss from a level the patient experienced before. In other words, if one always had trouble remembering names, the fact that one forgets them now is not a sign of Alzheimer's. The symptoms also begin gradually and continue to worsen, and doctors must rule out other causes.

To determine whether the patient has Alzheimer's, health care providers use a variety of tools. They speak with the patient and their family to learn about the symptoms, how daily functioning has changed, and the patient's medical history and overall health. Patients or their families may also fill out questionnaires. These generally include details about memory and thinking problems, changes in activity and behavior, and whether the patient is able to carry out everyday activities alone, with help, or not at all.

The evaluation includes neuropsychological testing—tests of different cognitive abilities, including memory, language, and problem solving. A physical examination and medical tests help determine whether something else could be causing the dementia. For example, blood tests may reveal vitamin deficiencies or infections. Psychiatrist William Klunk, codirector of the University of Pittsburgh Alzheimer Disease Research Center, summarized what patients experienced in a dementia evaluation at that facility:

*In a three- or four-hour evaluation, they get a series of neuropsychological tests that test a variety of different cognitive functions—memory, visual-spatial function, executive function, language function, all of these things. They're seen by a neurologist to see if they have other neurological symptoms that might be involved. They're seen by a psychiatrist to look for depression and other co-morbidities [additional, related medical problems]. Their basic physical health is evaluated to see if there's something that could be causing the memory impairment. After this evaluation, we look for a typical constellation of current symptoms and a typical history of development symptoms.*[15]

Brain imaging—generally magnetic resonance imaging (MRI), which uses a magnetic field and sound waves to create a computerized image, or a computerized tomography (CT) scan, also sometimes called a computerized axial tomography (CAT) scan, which puts together many X-rays to form a cross-sectional image—is part of the evaluation. This could reveal damage that resulted from some other cause, such as vascular problems, or it could reveal the type of damage doctors would expect to see from Alzheimer's. Klunk explained, "What we're typically looking for is the absence of tumors or strokes, and the presence of brain shrinkage in a specific pattern."[16] Doctors may repeat tests to see how the symptoms change over time.

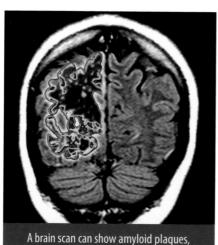

A brain scan can show amyloid plaques, but since many people with plaques do not have Alzheimer's, it cannot be the only tool doctors use to diagnose the disease.

The information collected during the dementia evaluation helps doctors make a diagnosis. In research clinics, investigators use the terms "probable" and "possible" Alzheimer's. Possible Alzheimer's means the dementia symptoms could be caused by Alzheimer's, but they could also be caused by another problem that the evaluation has revealed. Lopez explained, "The term 'possible' is commonly used when the patient has some other illness that can also cause cognitive problems. For example, a person can have a stroke that affects his/her cognitive abilities, and Alzheimer's disease. Therefore, the word 'possible' indicates that the patient has two conditions that can affect cognition."[17] If no other cause is found, the diagnosis is probable Alzheimer's. The diagnosis is worded that way because even though doctors can diagnose Alzheimer's with 90 percent accuracy, they cannot give a definite diagnosis without examining the brain after death. Outside of research clinics, doctors may not always distinguish between possible and probable Alzheimer's.

Instead of Alzheimer's, the diagnosis could be mild cognitive impairment (MCI). People with this condition have greater memory problems than are normal for their age but not as severe as the memory problems of people with dementia. There are two types of MCI: amnestic MCI, which mainly affects memory, and nonamnestic MCI, which affects things other than memory. According to the Alzheimer's Association, "Thinking skills that may be affected by nonamnestic MCI include the ability to make sound [logical] decisions, judge the time or sequence of steps needed to complete a complex task, or visual perception."[18] Generally, the symptoms of both types do not interfere with a person's daily activities. For some people with MCI, the symptoms stay the same or even improve. For others, the problems progress until they develop Alzheimer's or another dementia. People with MCI are at greater risk for developing Alzheimer's than people without it.

Researchers still do not understand why some people with MCI develop Alzheimer's and others do not.

One hypothesis is that, for some patients, MCI may be a form of preclinical Alzheimer's—a very early stage in which the symptoms have not yet progressed enough to allow doctors to diagnose the problem. For other patients, MCI may have other causes, such as depression, stroke, side effect of medication, or another illness.

## A Dangerous Stigma

Like many other diseases and disorders that mainly affect the brain, Alzheimer's has a stigma, or negative image, attached to it. This stigma is especially strong in Western cultures, where a person often measures their own worth and the worth of others by their intelligence and ability to contribute to society. The fear of losing independence and being seen as unintelligent is sometimes strong enough to stop people from seeking a diagnosis or even discussing the matter. Unfortunately, this can have dangerous effects on the patient as well as their loved ones. According to Angela Lunde, the cognitive health and wellness director at a senior living community,

> *If stigma makes a person with memory concerns resist seeing a doctor, then they're losing out on the benefits offered by timely treatments, therapies, and programs. If stigma prevents caregivers from seeking support from family and friends, as well as formal services, then ultimately there can be additional negative outcomes for these caregivers—increased burden, stress, depression, and physical illness.*[19]

It is important for people to remember that not being diagnosed does not make the disease go away; whether they hear it from a doctor or not, they still have Alzheimer's. Delaying diagnosis only prevents someone from getting the treatment they need until it is too late.

Sometimes people are not afraid of being

diagnosed, but their symptoms are mild enough that their doctors miss them or the symptoms may not be apparent during the appointment. For people who are concerned about getting an early diagnosis, there is an at-home test that can be downloaded for free from the website of the Ohio State University Wexner Medical Center. The test, which is called the Self-Administered Gerocognitive Examination (SAGE), was developed in 2009 by Dr. Douglas W. Scharre, a neurologist at the Wexner Center.

People who are concerned about their cognitive abilities can take the SAGE test.

An early diagnosis carries many benefits. It allows doctors to determine the true cause of the problem so they can address it properly. In a few cases, the cause turns out to be something that is reversible with proper treatment. In other cases, the condition may not reverse, but it will not get worse if the patient seeks treatment in time.

Even if the diagnosis is Alzheimer's, treatment is most effective if it is started early. The drugs used to treat Alzheimer's cannot reverse the damage or cure the disease, but they can help preserve the patient's mental functioning for months or years longer than would have been the case without them. The diagnosis can help prevent problems by putting family members on the alert at an early stage. For example, once family members know about the situation, they can remind the person with Alzheimer's to take needed medications.

An early diagnosis also allows people with Alzheimer's to make plans and be involved with decisions about the future while they are still able. They can plan where they will live when they can no longer care for themselves and how their financial matters will be handled. They may also decide to participate in research studies to help doctors understand the causes of Alzheimer's and develop better treatments for the future.

## Withholding Information: An Unethical Decision

The stigma surrounding Alzheimer's is so strong that it even affects many doctors. In 2015, *TIME* magazine reported that 45 percent of people who were given treatment for Alzheimer's were never told by their doctors that they had the disease. These patients were billed for their treatment but were not informed what it was for. When asked, many doctors said they did not tell their patients the diagnosis because they were worried about upsetting the patient or they did not have time to fully explain it. Since Alzheimer's can only be verified with an autopsy, or surgery after death, some doctors also worry about accidentally misdiagnosing a patient and causing them fear for no reason.

Although it is understandable that a doctor might wish to avoid upsetting their patient, keeping the diagnosis a secret is seen by many as unethical, or morally wrong, even if the doctors are not withholding medical treatment from the patient. People have a right to know their own medical condition, and being aware of their diagnosis can help them and their loved ones make important decisions.

Family and friends who will serve as caregivers for the person with Alzheimer's also benefit from having time to learn about the disease. They can set up a support system in advance and learn ways to deal with upcoming difficulties. Many challenges arise from living with Alzheimer's, both for patients and for caregivers, but working together to create a plan can minimize those difficulties.

## CHAPTER THREE

# THE SCIENCE BEHIND ALZHEIMER'S

Over the years, researchers have studied the brain in an effort to understand how the changes that take place because of Alzheimer's affect it. Although they know what happens in a brain that has Alzheimer's, researchers, in many cases, do not know exactly why those changes affect memory and personality. Additionally, they are not completely sure why these changes occur in the first place. Discovering this information might make it easier to develop medications to treat Alzheimer's because researchers will have a better idea of which parts of the brain to target.

## How a Healthy Brain Works

A healthy human brain contains 100 billion nerve cells, or neurons. Each neuron has a cell body with a long, narrow "arm" called an axon for sending messages to other neurons. Each neuron also has thin extensions called dendrites branching out from it to receive messages from other neurons. To send a message, a neuron transmits an electrical signal along its axon. The axon then releases chemicals called neurotransmitters, which carry the message across the synapse. When these chemical messengers reach the next neuron, they fit into receptors on that neuron the way a key fits into a lock. Most receptors are on the dendrites, but some are also on the cell body. The signal that the neurotransmitters deliver passes through the

## How Do Neurons Work?

- An electrical impulse runs down the axon.

- This causes the axon to release chemical messengers, or neurotransmitters.

- The neurotransmitters travel across the synapse. Each neuron has about 1,000 synapses between its axon and the dendrites of other neurons.

- The neurotransmitters reach a dendrite of the next neuron.

- The neurotransmitters fit into receptors on the dendrite in order to deliver their message.

receiving neuron, which then sends the message along its axon and on to other neurons. All of this happens in the blink of an eye.

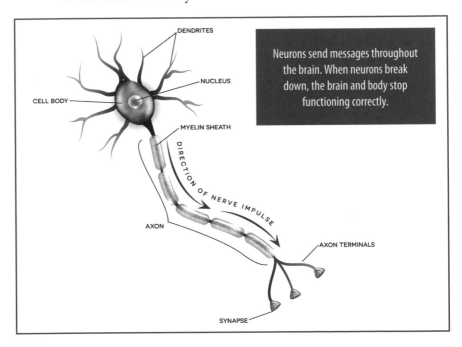

Neurons send messages throughout the brain. When neurons break down, the brain and body stop functioning correctly.

Neurons need oxygen, nutrients, and other chemicals to make energy, build proteins, and repair themselves. Blood delivers these materials to the brain as it travels through a network of large blood vessels called arteries that branch off into smaller arteries called arterioles, which branch off again into tiny vessels called capillaries. The brain's transportation network has 400 billion capillaries. The blood also carries away waste products. Between 20 and 25 percent of all the blood a human heart pumps is directed to the brain.

## Solving a Mystery

Researchers once believed the amyloid plaques that form in a brain with Alzheimer's were what caused the damage to the neurons. Now, many think the true culprit is smaller clusters of amyloid beta (which scientists sometimes abbreviate as Aβ) called oligomers. These may cause the damage by interfering with the signals between neurons. The brain may clump the oligomers together into plaques in an effort to get rid of them. The University of Pittsburgh's William Klunk compared plaques to toxic waste dumps.

Even healthy brains produce some amount of Aβ. Why it forms oligomers and plaques in some brains and not in others is not completely understood. In the past, researchers believed the brains of people with Alzheimer's made more Aβ than the brains of people who never developed the disease. They assumed that since there was more Aβ in the brain, it would eventually clump up into plaques. However, LiveScience reported in 2010 that new studies suggested everyone's brain makes about the same amount of Aβ, but the brains of people who develop Alzheimer's are less able to clear it out over time. These findings are important because they may help doctors diagnose Alzheimer's before symptoms appear and could give drug developers a better idea of what their medications should target.

Unlike plaques, which form between neurons, neurofibrillary tangles form inside neurons. Each neuron has microscopic tubes that extend down its axon. The neuron transports its nutrients, neurotransmitters, and other materials through these tubes. A chemical called a tau protein binds to the tubes to keep their structure strong and stable.

Normally, these threads of tau protein have phosphorus molecules attached to them. Phosphorus is a mineral that is important to keep a body functioning properly; some of its jobs include filtering waste and repairing cells. However, in a brain with Alzheimer's, a greater amount of phosphorus attaches to the tau. This causes the tau threads to unstick from the tubes they were helping support. A loose tau thread becomes entangled with other loose tau threads to form the neurofibrillary tangles Alois Alzheimer described. As a result, the tubes collapse. With its transport system disrupted, the neuron can no longer move materials or communicate with other neurons. These damaged neurons soon die.

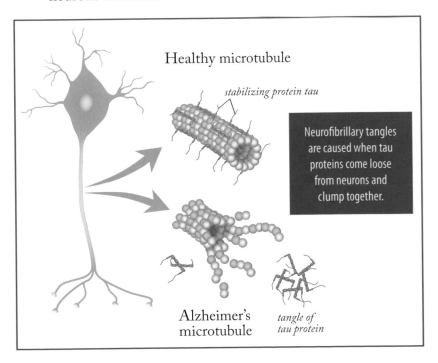

Healthy microtubule

*stabilizing protein tau*

Neurofibrillary tangles are caused when tau proteins come loose from neurons and clump together.

Alzheimer's microtubule

*tangle of tau protein*

## The Role of Genetics

One factor that makes the situation even more confusing is that some people who accumulate Aβ in their brains do not develop Alzheimer's symptoms. Researchers who are conducting studies with new brain imaging techniques are finding plaques in healthy, living people. Pathologists who conduct autopsies also find plaques in patients who have died from other causes and showed no signs of Alzheimer's while they were alive. Some experts say there are clearly certain factors protecting some brains from the effects of the plaques, but more research is needed to determine what those factors are. However, others disagree. According to Dr. David Holtzman, chairman of the department of neurology at Washington University School of Medicine in St. Louis, Missouri, it can take up to 15 years before plaques start having a negative effect on the brain. He and others believe some healthy elderly people who are found to have plaques in their brain would have started to show Alzheimer's symptoms eventually. Again, more research is needed to see which theory is correct.

What scientists do know is that Alzheimer's is caused by a combination of genetic and lifestyle factors. Genetic factors are things people cannot control; for example, someone whose parents or grandparents had Alzheimer's has a higher risk of getting the disease. Early-onset Alzheimer's appears to have more to do with genetics. Researchers have found mutations in three different chromosomes, which are long strings of genes that are coiled up into packages inside cells. Normally, people inherit 23 chromosomes from their mother and 23 from their father, for a total of 46, or 23 pairs of chromosomes. One pair of these chromosomes determines whether the person is male or female. The other pairs are identified by numbers—from 1 to 22.

Each chromosome contains thousands of genes. These genes give cells instructions on how to make proteins. If a mutation, or permanent change in a gene, occurs, the instructions are delivered incorrectly, and the cells may make an abnormal form of the protein. In some families, researchers have found, people with Alzheimer's inherited gene mutations on chromosome 21. In others, a mutation occurred on chromosome 14 or chromosome 1.

All of these mutations affect production of Aβ, the protein pieces that clump together to form plaques between neurons. The mutations on chromosome 21 instruct cells to make an abnormal form of the larger protein that Aβ comes from. The mutations on chromosomes 14 and 1 affect an enzyme that snips this larger protein into smaller pieces to release Aβ.

The discovery that genetic mutations cause early-onset Alzheimer's in certain families was a breakthrough, but it did not explain other cases of early-onset Alzheimer's. It also did not explain late-onset Alzheimer's. People who develop late-onset Alzheimer's do not have the gene mutations on chromosomes 1, 14, or 21. Researchers have not found a gene that by itself causes late-onset Alzheimer's, but they have found certain genes that appear to increase a person's risk for developing the disease.

So far, the only gene found to have a significant effect on a person's chances of developing late-onset Alzheimer's is a gene on chromosome 19. Because this gene contains instructions for making a protein called apolipoprotein E (APOE), it is known as the APOE gene. It can take several different forms, and each form is associated with a different level of risk of a person developing Alzheimer's.

## Lifestyle Factors

Lifestyle factors also play a role in a person's risk for developing Alzheimer's. Unlike genes, these are things most people are able to control. One lifestyle factor is sleep. Scientists believe sleep is necessary to clear away waste material from the brain, including getting rid of Aβ before it can form oligomers. Another is diet. Researchers have found that type 2 diabetes, which can be caused by obesity, is one risk factor for dementia. Another is a high glycemic diet, which means a diet high in carbohydrates that cause blood sugar to rise quickly, such as potatoes, sugar, flour, rice, and cookies. According to Alzheimer's Research UK,

> *In one study of nearly 500 middle aged people, researchers found that those with a high glycaemic diet had faster rates of memory decline over two years. They also found that a high glycaemic diet was associated with brain shrinkage on an MRI scan, indicating damage in the brain. From this particular study, it is not possible to conclude that diet is driving these changes in the brain, but it does raise the importance of exploring the link between diet, diabetes, and dementia.*[20]

A diet that includes a lot of foods with a high glycemic index, such as the ones shown here, may increase a person's risk of developing Alzheimer's.

Additionally, scientists have known for a long time that keeping the brain active—for example, by doing crossword puzzles or studying new things—decreases the risk of getting Alzheimer's. However, whatever the cause of Alzheimer's, the results are clear. Communication between neurons is lost, and damaged neurons die. As more neurons die in a certain brain area, that area atrophies, or shrinks. The fluid-filled spaces, or ventricles, between brain areas enlarge. The person gradually loses memory and other thinking abilities, and the symptoms get worse as physical damage spreads to other areas. Since different brain areas handle different tasks, not all abilities are affected at the same time.

## More Than One Kind of Memory

Different brain areas handle different types of memory, and Alzheimer's does not damage all of these at the same time. Short-term memory allows a person to recall information for a few seconds up to a few hours. It includes the ability to recall recent events, such as where a person parked the car or whether they turned on the stove. In Alzheimer's, the damage begins in brain areas involved with short-term memory.

Long-term memory is affected later, when the damage has spread to other parts of the brain. There are several different parts of long-term memory that may all be affected at different times by Alzheimer's. Semantic memory involves knowledge of facts, concepts, and words. For example, semantic memory allows a person to recite the alphabet or remember who George Washington was. Episodic memory stores a person's experiences and life events. When this type of memory is damaged, a person may no longer be able to recall things such as what happened on their wedding day or how they felt when their first child was born. Implicit, or procedural, memory allows a person to recall information stored in the subconscious in order to perform familiar tasks automatically. This type of memory allows a person to do such things as ride a bike, drive a car, get dressed, or make a sandwich without having to consciously think about how to do it every time.

Healthy brains also store certain things in prospective memory, which includes things that need to be remembered in the future. This is why people with Alzheimer's sometimes do not remember where they put things; the location of the item does not get properly stored in the person's prospective memory.

## Making It Worse

While scientists try to learn more about how plaques and tangles damage the brain, they also investigate other factors that could worsen the damage. Some believe that inflammation—an immune system reaction to infection or injury—increases the damage once Alzheimer's has begun. The immune system recognizes the plaques in the brain as invaders and attacks them. This causes inflammation, which releases chemicals that can further damage the brain. Another idea is that free radicals—oxygen and nitrogen molecules that combine easily with other molecules—damage neurons. Doctors have also identified several things that may make the symptoms of Alzheimer's progress more quickly, although some of these can be reversed once a doctor is aware of the problem. These include:

- *Infections, such as pneumonia, a urinary tract infection, or a sinus infection*
- *Reaction to some prescription medications*
- *Fatigue or lack of sleep*
- *Social or environmental changes, such as moving or the presence of new medical care staff or family members*
- *Vitamin deficiencies, including B12, thiamin, niacin, and folate*
- *Depression*
- *Thyroid problems*
- *Additional neurological conditions*[21]

Doctors cannot reverse the damage done by Alzheimer's, but they have developed medications that help Alzheimer's sufferers preserve their mental functioning for months or years longer. In addition, researchers are trying to learn what prompts the damage to begin in the first place.

## CHAPTER FOUR

# TREATMENT FOR ALZHEIMER'S

The research that scientists have done on the causes of Alzheimer's has led to the development of improved treatments. However, it takes a long time for a medication to become available because it must go through multiple clinical trials to make sure it is safe for humans to take, will actually help the problem, and will not have side effects that are worse than the disease. This means treatments based off recent discoveries may not be available for many years. In the meantime, there are medications that have already passed their trials that can slow the symptoms of Alzheimer's for a few years.

## Targeting the Synapses

Medications currently used to treat Alzheimer's target a problem that occurs at the synapses between neurons. Klunk explained, "Synapses are sites where brain cells communicate with each other. That's a critical event in the brain. And they do that communication through chemical messengers."[22] One of these chemical messengers, or neurotransmitters, is acetylcholine, which helps the brain form memories.

In the 1970s, when awareness about Alzheimer's was rising, researchers discovered that levels of acetylcholine were lower in people with the disease. The reason is that an enzyme (a protein that speeds up a chemical reaction) called acetylcholinesterase breaks down acetylcholine. This prevents the neurotransmitter from delivering its message.

This discovery led scientists to develop drugs that stop or slow down this enzyme to prevent it from interfering with communication between neurons. These drugs are called cholinesterase inhibitors. Although the drugs' actions in the brain are not completely understood, Klunk explained how doctors believe they address the problem:

> *Usually one neuron shoots out acetylcholine onto its neighboring neuron, the neighboring neuron gets the message, and the acetylcholinesterase of the synaptic cleft chews up the rest of the message and the message is over. Well, it's sort of crude, but if you inhibit that acetylcholinesterase enzyme, then the message stays there longer. And it has more of an effect. And even though that isn't an exact replacement for the physiology [the brain's natural function], it still can be beneficial.[23]*

## Mild to Moderate Alzheimer's Treatments

The first medication that the U.S. Food and Drug Administration (FDA) approved for treating Alzheimer's symptoms was tacrine (brand name Cognex) in 1993. Doctors prescribed this cholinesterase inhibitor for mild to moderate Alzheimer's. It is no longer used because its side effects, which include possible liver damage, are more serious than those of cholinesterase inhibitors that were developed later. Another disadvantage is that it had to be taken four times a day, compared with once or twice a day for others.

Over the following years, the FDA approved three other cholinesterase inhibitors that doctors currently prescribe for Alzheimer's. In 1996, donepezil (Aricept) was approved for mild to moderate Alzheimer's and was later also approved for severe Alzheimer's. Rivastigmine (Exelon), which was approved in 2000, and galantamine (Razadyne), approved in 2001, treat mild to moderate Alzheimer's.

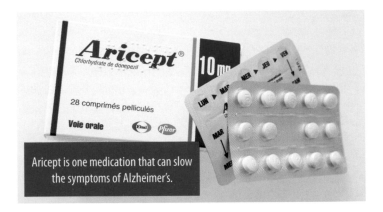

Aricept is one medication that can slow the symptoms of Alzheimer's.

Cholinesterase inhibitors do not cure Alzheimer's or reverse the damage, but they may allow people with the disease to preserve their mental functioning longer. Neurologist Oscar Lopez pointed out, "They are not magic pills. They are not restoring function; they are symptomatic treatments. And they do what they're supposed to do—slow down progression."[24] In patients with Alzheimer's for whom cholinesterase inhibitors prove effective, the drugs keep symptoms from worsening for an average of six to twelve months. A minority of patients appear to benefit longer. All cholinesterase inhibitors work in the same way, but an individual patient may respond better to one than to another.

## Severe Alzheimer's Treatments

While cholinesterase inhibitors help increase levels of the chemical messenger acetylcholine, a different type of medication helps regulate levels of another chemical messenger. Glutamate is also a neurotransmitter involved with memory. Neurons damaged by Alzheimer's release larger than normal amounts of glutamate. When glutamate attaches itself to receptors on a neuron in order to deliver its message, it allows calcium to enter that neuron. The calcium plays a role in helping the neuron store information. If glutamate levels are too high, an unhealthy amount of calcium enters the neuron and contributes to damage.

In 2003, the FDA approved memantine (Namenda), a drug developed to address this problem. Later, it also approved Namzaric, which is a combination of memantine and donepezil. Doctors believe memantine protects neurons by blocking glutamate from entering these receptors. They prescribe it to patients with moderate to severe Alzheimer's. As with the cholinesterase inhibitors, memantine does not cure Alzheimer's or reverse the damage, but it can help slow progression of the disease. A patient can take both memantine and a cholinesterase inhibitor at the same time. As with all medications, there are side effects, but these tend to be mild, and not everyone will experience them. They include nausea, dizziness, vomiting, and diarrhea.

## Treating the Symptoms

Cholinesterase inhibitors and memantine are the only drugs specifically approved for treating Alzheimer's. Other drugs are available for treating problems with mood and behavior that often arise in patients with Alzheimer's. Between 70 and 90 percent of patients experience behavioral symptoms. Experts recommend trying non-drug approaches first, such as keeping the person comfortable, distracting them with an activity, making sure they get plenty of rest, responding to the person's requests, and developing effective communication. However, if these strategies fail or if the symptoms create a dangerous situation, doctors generally prescribe medications.

Depression is common in people with Alzheimer's. Doctors may prescribe one of several different antidepressant medications to address the problem. Some of the most common ones are classified as selective serotonin reuptake inhibitors (SSRIs) because they help regulate levels of the neurotransmitter serotonin. Low serotonin levels are associated with depression; SSRIs stop the brain from reabsorbing too much serotonin after it has been released.

Problems such as agitation, aggression, hallucinations, and delusions can cause much distress for people with Alzheimer's and for their caregivers. Doctors often prescribe antipsychotic medications to control hallucinations and delusions in people with other disorders, and these medications may also help control agitation and other mood problems. In people with dementia, however, antipsychotics have been found to carry an increased risk of stroke and death.

For patients who are restless, anxious, and show disruptive behavior, some doctors prescribe an anxiolytic medicine. The most common types of anxiolytics are benzodiazepines; these include alprazolam (Xanax), clonazepam (Klonopin), and diazepam (Valium). However, these medications are known to be addictive, so they are generally prescribed for short-term use and should not be given to a patient with Alzheimer's unless absolutely necessary. Benzodiazepines work by boosting the effectiveness of the neurotransmitter gamma-aminobutyric acid (GABA), which reduces stress and anxiety. They tend to make people sleepy, so they are sometimes also used to treat sleep problems—another common issue with Alzheimer's.

When people with Alzheimer's cannot sleep through the night, this can create a dangerous situation. For instance, they may wander, turn on the stove, or get into other dangerous situations while caregivers are sleeping. This adds to the stress on caregivers and often prevents them from getting a good night's sleep themselves. Strategies for handling the problem include keeping the same bedtime every night, helping the person stay active earlier in the day, and limiting caffeine. Sleeping aids may increase confusion in people with Alzheimer's,

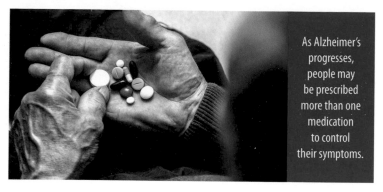

As Alzheimer's progresses, people may be prescribed more than one medication to control their symptoms.

especially if these interact with other medications the person is taking. Some sleeping aids lead to physical dependence. For these reasons, doctors generally prescribe sleeping aids to patients with Alzheimer's only after nondrug strategies have failed.

## Nondrug Treatments

Another strategy for managing symptoms is regular exercise. Studies show that exercise helps preserve cognitive abilities, and it also improves mood and helps fight depression. Exercise earlier in the day can help combat sleep problems because the person will feel tired at night. It also improves overall physical health.

People with Alzheimer's may find exercise a challenge, but exercise does not have to be strenuous to have good results. It can be as simple as a short walk with a caregiver. When people with Alzheimer's and their caregivers exercise together, both experience healthful results.

Other nonmedical therapies can enrich the lives of people with Alzheimer's. Because of the damage Alzheimer's causes to the brain, people with this disease often have trouble communicating, and they may no longer be able to participate in activities they once enjoyed. Patients with Alzheimer's benefit from activities that bring meaning to their lives and that allow them to interact with other people.

Art is often used as a therapy. Painting, drawing, or

simple craft projects can give people with Alzheimer's a sense of accomplishment and a way to express themselves. Music therapy helps people relax as well as improving sleep and other behavioral problems. It includes music familiar to the person, perhaps from the past. People with Alzheimer's are encouraged to participate by singing and moving to the music.

Because people with Alzheimer's may still remember details from the past when the present has become confusing, reminiscence therapy can be comforting. It involves activities such as looking at old photographs, watching old movies or television shows the person once enjoyed, and asking the person to tell about events from the past.

Reading to the person can also provide enjoyment. Some short books have been written especially for people who have dementia. Peter V. Rabins, the former codirector of the Division of Geriatric Psychiatry and Neuropsychiatry at the Johns Hopkins University School of Medicine, noted, "Anything that helps make it easier for people to interact produces benefits in both directions—the family member with the disease and the caregiver. It gives the person with the disease a chance to interact with grandkids or younger children. It's positive both ways."[25]

Some less common therapies include aromatherapy, which uses certain smells to relax people; light therapy, which involves exposing the person to bright light and may help treat increased agitation in the evenings;

Looking at old photographs with family members may be good therapy for someone with Alzheimer's.

and doll therapy, which involves giving a person with Alzheimer's a doll to take care of. Doll therapy can give some patients a sense of control and independence without exposing a child to potential danger.

## The Risks of Alternative Treatments

Some people believe natural remedies—including certain herbs, spices, and vitamins—should be used either instead of or along with medications. Many people will try anything they think will help them or their loved one with Alzheimer's, but experts warn people to be careful about spending money on remedies that are unproven. Some things, such as omega-3 fatty acids, curcumin, and ginkgo, have been found to have no effect on delaying or reversing Alzheimer's. One product called coral calcium has been heavily marketed as a miraculous cure for Alzheimer's despite having no real effect, causing the FDA to file complaints against people who sell it. The complaints will hopefully stop them from taking advantage of people who are in a vulnerable situation.

Other products may actually be dangerous for people with Alzheimer's. Dietary supplements are not regulated by the FDA the way medicine and food are, so some may have unknown impurities or ingredients that are not listed on the label. One product called coenzyme Q10 can be harmful when too much is taken, and no testing has been done to determine how much is "too much." Huperzine A, a moss extract that has effects similar to cholinesterase inhibitors, is sold as a dietary supplement, but it can have dangerous interactions with other Alzheimer's drugs. People who have Alzheimer's should always discuss treatment with their doctors before trying any new products and should avoid anything that promises dramatic or speedy results.

## A Sad Reality

Although the treatments that are currently available can help someone with Alzheimer's stay active and focused for longer than they would without the medications, the sad fact is that nothing will reverse Alzheimer's once it has started. At a certain point, if the person lives long enough, their medication will stop working. Even with medication, the patient and their loved ones will need to adjust to a new way of doing things.

## CHAPTER FIVE

# MAKING ADJUSTMENTS

Alzheimer's disease affects not just the patient but their loved ones as well. As the disease progresses, the patient requires one or more caregivers because they will no longer be able to do everyday activities such as cook, drive, or dress themselves. Since there is currently no cure for Alzheimer's, this caregiving will need to continue for the rest of the person's life. Some families can afford to hire in-home nurses, but even if they do this, the nurses are not there every hour of the day; a family member or friend generally needs to be willing to take care of the patient the rest of the time.

Caregiving can be challenging because it requires a lot of time and energy. Additionally, the personality changes Alzheimer's often causes may make the patient frustrating to deal with; for instance, they may insist they do not need help when they clearly do. For these reasons, it is important for caregivers to share responsibility with others and make sure they take care of themselves as well.

## Unwanted Dependence

A big challenge for many people with Alzheimer's is coming to terms with the idea of losing their independence. Mary Ann Becklenberg, who was diagnosed with Alzheimer's at age 62, said, "Prior to having this disease, I wasn't a person who needed to ask for help much. But now I do, and it's been a blow to my self-assurance and self-esteem. I can't participate fully in life like I used to, and it's a huge loss."[26]

Seventy percent of people with Alzheimer's and other dementias live at home, where they receive help and care from family and friends. Others live in institutional settings, such as nursing homes or extended-care facilities. Studies show that around 94 percent of unpaid caregivers are relatives of the person with Alzheimer's, while the others are friends.

Some people hire in-home caregivers, but the majority of people with Alzheimer's have at least one family member as a full- or part-time caregiver.

The caregiver's role depends on the situation and needs of the person with Alzheimer's. This role can change as the disease progresses. Besides making sure that the person with Alzheimer's takes medications and pays bills at the right time, caregivers help with shopping, cooking, and transportation. They arrange for medical care, try to handle any behavioral problems that arise, and keep the person with Alzheimer's safe from danger. Eventually, they need to help the person with everyday tasks such as dressing, bathing, and using the bathroom. Some caregivers take responsibility for the person 24 hours a day, 7 days a week.

## Becoming Forgetful

As the mild forgetfulness of early Alzheimer's progresses to more severe memory loss, both the person with Alzheimer's and caregivers can become frustrated.

People with Alzheimer's often ask the same question over and over. They remember certain details but forget others, or they remember something today that they were unable to remember yesterday and will be unable to remember tomorrow. Because the disease strikes recent memory first, they may recall seemingly unimportant details from years ago but forget important information from the present. For example, they may forget current family members but remember the name of their first-grade teacher.

Family and friends often feel hurt or distressed when their loved one fails to remember them. They may also feel frustrated at having to answer the same questions repeatedly. Experts recommend keeping in mind that these problems are caused by the disease and that Alzheimer's sufferers cannot choose what or when they will remember.

Many caregivers report that keeping a sense of humor helps everyone cope. Kathy Hatfield created a blog called *KnowItAlz* after she began caring for her father, who had Alzheimer's. Many of her posts described funny moments she and her father shared even after his diagnosis. For example:

> *Dad has the same breakfast every day. It consists of a bowl of bran cereal, a banana, and a glass of orange juice. Yesterday, he got up, ate breakfast, and headed to the shower. When he emerged from the bathroom, he asked me if he had already eaten, and I responded with a simple, "yes." He bowed his head and glumly replied, "I can't believe I can't remember eating breakfast. My mind must be completely gone." Dad was really sad and worried, so I said, "If you can't remember, you had Fillet Mignon, Eggs Benedict, sourdough toast with real butter and a big glass of champagne for breakfast." He laughed so hard, he forgot that he was frustrated. Laughter is the best therapy; for both of us!*[27]

# Finding New Ways to Communicate

As memory and other thinking abilities decline, communication becomes more difficult. People with Alzheimer's may start a sentence and forget what they were trying to say, or they may have trouble finding the right words. They may repeat the same words over and over again even when those words have nothing to do with the current situation. When others speak, people with Alzheimer's may have trouble understanding the meaning of words or paying attention. These problems can frustrate the person with Alzheimer's, who is struggling to be understood, and the caregivers, who are struggling to understand and to get their own points across. In the case of people who spoke a different language as a child, the challenge may become even greater; because Alzheimer's first robs more recent memories while leaving old ones intact, these people may begin to speak and understand only their original language.

By being careful about the way they word sentences, caregivers may be able to improve communication. If they offer simple instructions, one step at a time, this may help the person with Alzheimer's complete tasks. Since the person may have trouble understanding the meaning of words, repeating a thought in different words sometimes helps. Questions that can be answered with a yes or no or ones offering only two choices are easier for someone with Alzheimer's to answer. For example, in the guide *Caring for a Person with Alzheimer's Disease*, the National

It can be frustrating for caregivers when a person with Alzheimer's refuses care, but rather than forcing the person to do something, the caregiver should find a new way to communicate.

Institute on Aging suggests asking, "Are you tired?" instead of "How do you feel?" and "Would you like a hamburger or chicken for dinner?" instead of "What would you like for dinner?"[28]

Patiently allowing time for the person with Alzheimer's to complete their thought helps communication and shows respect. Interrupting or speaking about the person to others as if the person was not there only adds to their frustration. Nonverbal communication, such as facial expressions, gestures, or a touch on the arm, can also help get ideas across. Finding an effective way to communicate is important because when a person with Alzheimer's feels confused by what is being asked of them or does not like the way they are being talked to, they may refuse to do something they need to do. When this happens, some caregivers may think they need to simply force the patient to do what they want, especially if it is something necessary such as eating or taking a shower. However, the Social Care Institute for Excellence (SCIE), an organization that offers information to people who use caregiver services, explained why this should not be done:

> *Trying to force a person with dementia to accept personal care constitutes abuse. It is a fundamental human right to say 'no.' However, neglecting someone's personal care needs can also be abusive, as the person's health may be put at risk. Therefore, it is essential to understand the person's reasons for refusing and to address this.*

> *We may need to find an alternative way of providing the personal care the person needs, for example, by offering a bath rather than a shower ... Perhaps the person always had a bath on Sunday mornings and had stand-up washes for the rest of the week. Then we need to adapt to this routine. Through finding out this background information, observing,*

*and listening to the person with dementia, we can gradually build up a picture of the personal care routines and preferences of each individual.*[29]

In some cases where the patient's health would not be harmed, caregivers may feel a person's refusal to do something is unacceptable because it makes caregiving more time consuming; to use the example given above, they may not want to take the time to give someone a bath rather than a shower. In other cases, it may be because they feel they know what is best for the patient—for example, the person with Alzheimer's may want to stay up until 11:00 p.m., but the caregiver may want them to go to bed at 9:00 p.m. In situations such as these, rather than using physical force or forceful language—both of which, in addition to violating the patient's rights, are likely to make them refuse even more strongly—the caregiver should speak gently to the patient, try to find out how they are feeling, and see if there is a way a compromise can be reached.

## Behavioral Changes

Besides problems with memory and communication, many different personality and behavioral changes can arise in a person who has Alzheimer's. These may include aggression, poor impulse control (for example, not knowing when to stop drinking alcohol), wandering, paranoia (believing people wish them harm), forgetting to take care of hygiene, and inappropriate behavior such as undressing in public or shoplifting. Not everyone with Alzheimer's experiences these problems. Some may have a few mild problems or none at all. Others have catastrophic reactions. They become upset, and sometimes even violent, over matters that seem unimportant to others.

Many different factors can prompt these changes. The damage to the brain that Alzheimer's causes and

Some people with Alzheimer's experience paraonoia, which causes them to be fearful and suspicious of people for no reason.

the memory loss and confusion that go along with it can create feelings of anxiety, fear, or depression. These emotions can then trigger problem behaviors. Other factors, such as medications, illness, stress, and pain, can also have this effect. Figuring out what is behind the problem allows caregivers to address the cause and sometimes prevent the problem from happening again.

A common problem among people with Alzheimer's is agitation— a state of being worried, disturbed, and restless. Some people show their agitation by pacing back and forth. A change in routine, a new caregiver, or unfamiliar surroundings can create anxiety, fear, and confusion. These feelings, in turn, may trigger agitation. Pain, loneliness, lack of sleep, or other factors can also be at the root of the problem, as well as a reaction to the losses that people with Alzheimer's experience, such as the loss of a home, driver's license, or abilities that were important to them.

In some cases, agitation leads to aggressive behavior. The person may shout at or even hit others. Experts agree that such problems generally have a cause, and addressing that cause may help stop the problem. Psychiatrist Stephen Soreff offered an example based on his experience with nursing home residents: "When a resident with dementia contracts an infection, he may have difficulty telling others of his discomfort, and an aggressive outburst may be his way of communicating it. Based on our work in many long-term care facilities, we have found that unexpressed and unrecognized pain can lead to aggressive events."[30]

## Alzheimer's Disease Bill of Rights

In the 1990s, the Alzheimer's Bill of Rights was created by Virginia Bell and David Troxel, who have degrees in social work and public health, respectively. The document helped change the way people with Alzheimer's were treated. It states that people with Alzheimer's and other dementia deserve:

- To be informed of one's diagnosis

- To have appropriate, ongoing medical care

- To be treated as an adult, listened to, and afforded respect for one's feelings and point of view

- To be with individuals who know one's life story, including cultural and spiritual traditions

- To experience meaningful engagement throughout the day

- To live in a safe and stimulating environment

- To be outdoors on a regular basis

- To be free from psychotropic medications [medications that change brain chemistry] whenever possible

- To have welcomed physical contact, including hugging, caressing, and handholding

- To be an advocate for oneself and others

- To be part of a local, global, or online community

- To have care partners well trained in dementia care[1]

1. "The Best Friends™ Dementia Bill of Rights," Virginia Bell and David Troxel's Best Friends™ Approach to Alzheimer's and Dementia Care, 2013. bestfriendsapproach.com/about/the-best-friends-bill-of-rights/.

## Sundowning: A Nightly Problem

Sleep problems are also common for people with Alzheimer's. They may not want to go to bed or may have trouble sleeping through the night. This can add to the exhaustion of caregivers. Samara Howard, who quit her job to become a full-time caregiver for her mother, said, "Normally, I only sleep maybe two hours a night because she wakes up and she wanders and she turns on the stove."[31]

Sundowning, or increased agitation in the late afternoon or evening, can also disturb sleep patterns. Although it is unclear exactly why some people's symptoms get worse in the evening, experts' best guess is that since the body's natural inner clock is altered by the changes Alzheimer's causes in the brain, the fading light further disrupts it. They recommend keeping the person's surroundings well lit to address the problem. Other suggestions for dealing with sleep problems and sundowning are to limit caffeine, play soft music in the evening, make sure the person's bed is comfortable, and follow the same routine every day. Activities that take much effort, such as bathing, can be done early in the day so they do not create agitation in the evening.

## Wandering: When Walking Becomes Dangerous

An estimated six out of ten people with Alzheimer's will wander at some point. This can be dangerous for the person who wanders and terrifying for the caregivers. Often, people who wander are trying to return "home." They do not remember their current home and are looking for a place they lived decades earlier. Others are trying to go to work or to care for another responsibility that ended long ago. Since many have trouble communicating and may not even remember their names, they cannot ask for help when they get lost.

Even the most attentive caregiver will find it impossible to watch the person with Alzheimer's every minute of the day and night. Installing a system that chimes when a door opens or installing locks higher or lower than normal, where the person with Alzheimer's will have trouble seeing or reaching them, can prevent wandering. Sometimes disguising the door with a curtain or placing a mirror on the door prevents people with Alzheimer's from going outside. Caregivers can help the person deal with the urge to wander by reassuring them that everything is all right, sticking to a daily routine, and planning activities for times when wandering is most likely to happen.

Sometimes people with Alzheimer's start wandering and forget how to get home. This can be especially dangerous if they are not dressed correctly for the weather.

Caregivers can take measures ahead of time to make sure the person returns safely if they wander. They can let neighbors and local police know about the problem so everyone will be on the alert. An ID bracelet will ensure that anyone who finds the wanderer understands the problem and knows whom to call, even if the person with Alzheimer's cannot communicate. Caregivers can also enroll the person in the Alzheimer's Association Safe Return program, which provides 24-hour emergency help.

## Searching Storage Spaces and Hiding Objects

Some people with Alzheimer's search through closets, drawers, cupboards, or the refrigerator. This behavior is called rummaging; sometimes it results from boredom, and other times a person is searching for something they cannot name. They may also hide items around the house, which is known as hoarding. They may do this to try to keep a sense of control; when they are dependent on other people for most things, being the only one who knows where a particular item is may give them a feeling of independence. They may also hoard items if they become paranoid and fear that someone is trying to steal their possessions. This behavior is not always harmful, but it can create problems if the person hides needed or valuable items, especially if the items get put in the garbage can. It can also be a safety issue if the person rummages through dangerous items or finds spoiled food in the back of the refrigerator and eats it. This behavior can put stress on caregivers as they constantly clean up the rummaged areas or search for missing items. It can also cause an accidental invasion of the caregiver's privacy when a person with Alzheimer's rummages through drawers or cabinets where the caregiver keeps personal items.

Caregivers can minimize the problems hoarding and rummaging create by giving people with Alzheimer's their own special place to keep items.

To keep the person safe and minimize their own stress, caregivers may need to lock away dangerous items and be quick to throw away spoiled food. If the person hides or throws away mail, renting a post office box is one way to solve the problem. Providing the person with their own place to rummage, such as a cupboard or a box of objects that interests them, can also help. The National Institute on Aging gives further tips for dealing with rummaging and hoarding:

- *Keep the person with Alzheimer's from going into unused rooms. This limits his or her rummaging through and hiding things.*
- *Search the house to learn where the person often hides things. Once you find these places, check them often, out of sight of the person.*
- *Keep all trash cans covered or out of sight. People with Alzheimer's may not remember the purpose of the container or may rummage through it.*
- *Check trash containers before you empty them, in case something has been hidden there or thrown away by accident.*[32]

## Losing Touch with Reality

Patients with Alzheimer's sometimes experience hallucinations—imagining they see, hear, smell, feel, or taste something that is not real. The most common types of hallucinations involve sight and hearing. For example, the person may insist they hear music or see a long-dead relative present in the room. Hallucinations can be caused by Alzheimer's or by other factors, such as medication or another illness.

If the hallucinations do not bother the person, caregivers may not need to do anything to address them. Telling the person that the hallucination is not real only leads to an argument, so sometimes going along with the hallucinations is the best way to react. For example, Dr. Stephen Hoag took care of his mother, who had been a performer when she was younger. He described a typical trip to the grocery store with her after she developed Alzheimer's: "Mom would see all those people as an audience and say, 'You're on next!' So I'd take it away, singing and dancing with her and entertaining everyone."[33] On the other hand, if the person is upset or frightened by the hallucinations, caregivers can offer reassuring words or another activity for a distraction. Doctors can prescribe antipsychotic medications as a last resort if the hallucinations cause severe distress.

# Guilt: A Secret Side Effect

One thing many people do not speak about is the feeling of guilt some people experience when someone is diagnosed with Alzheimer's. Often this is an issue that affects caregivers, but anyone can experience guilt. For instance, a child may first be upset that their parent's personality is changing and then feel guilty because they know their parent cannot help this. *Today's Caregiver* magazine explained why people feel guilt and what they can do about it:

*You have a picture of the "Ideal You" with values you hold and how you relate to yourself and others. Guilt often arises when there's a mismatch between your day-to-day choices and the choices the "Ideal You" would have made … You may have needs out of line with this "Ideal You." You may believe that your own needs are insignificant, compared to the needs of your sick loved one. You then feel guilty when you recognize your needs, much less act upon them. A mother may ask herself, "How can I go out for a walk with my kids when my mother is at home in pain?" (A hint for this mother: she can give more to her mother with an open heart when she takes good care of herself.)*

*You may have feelings misaligned with the "Ideal You." Feeling angry about the injustice of your loved one's illness? You might even feel angry at your loved one for getting sick! Recognizing those feelings can produce a healthy dose of guilt. Yes, you may even feel guilty about feeling guilty.*[1]

Negative emotions, especially in difficult circumstances, are part of being human, and experiencing them does not make someone a bad person. There is no "right way" for a caregiver to feel. Recognizing the feelings, speaking with a friend or therapist about them, being kind to themselves, and meeting their own needs are all ways caregivers and other loved ones can deal with their negative emotions and minimize guilt.

1. Vicki Rackner, MD, "Eight Tips to Managing Caregiver Guilt," *Today's Caregiver*, accessed September 6, 2017. caregiver.com/articles/managing_caregiver_guilt/.

Delusions are different from hallucinations. With hallucinations, the person is being tricked by their senses; they actually are smelling or seeing something

People with Alzheimer's sometimes see or hear things no one else does.

that is not there. A delusion is a false belief—it is all in the mind, but it seems real to the person, so it can also create stress. This is especially true when the person with Alzheimer's becomes paranoid. The person may believe that a family member is trying to poison them or that a caregiver is stealing their possessions. This sometimes happens when the person with Alzheimer's hoards things and does not remember doing so.

Such false accusations can hurt and frustrate a care-giver, who is working hard to meets the person's needs. Experts urge caregivers not to take paranoia personal-ly but to remember that it is the result of damage from the disease. Psychiatrist and neuropathologist Richard Powers explained, "The content of the delusion has no basis on past life experiences. If the person is arguing about Mom cheating him or Sister stealing from him, people need to understand it isn't necessarily real. It's as if someone took a sledgehammer and smashed your computer and it starts printing out gobbledygook."[34] Instead of arguing about the accusation, offering to look for the item together or distracting the person with another activity brings better results.

Trying to imagine the situation from the patient's point of view can help caregivers understand why a person with Alzheimer's may react in a way that seems illogical to healthy people. Beth Kallmyer, vice president of constituent services for the Alzheimer's Association, said, "Imagine that you go to get your wallet right where you left it and it's gone. You positively know you didn't move it—because you have no memory of doing that. So the only logical conclusion is that someone else did. That's the reality from the perspective of a person with dementia."[35]

## Caregivers Need Care, Too

Besides its devastating effects on people who have the disease, Alzheimer's takes a heavy toll on caregivers. Caregivers of people with Alzheimer's and other dementias generally spend more time in their role than caregivers of people with other illnesses, and the care continues for years. Caregivers who have parents with Alzheimer's often find themselves trying to care for their children and their aging parent at the same time. Spouses and siblings of people with Alzheimer's may be older and struggling to deal with their own health problems along with caring for their loved one.

In addition to the exhaustion that often goes along with their role, caregivers experience the grief of seeing their loved one's health and mental abilities decline. "It's saddening and disheartening to watch someone you love disappear like that,"[36] commented Greg Kalkwarf, whose grandfather died of Alzheimer's and whose mother has it as well. Caregivers often suffer from stress, anxiety, and depression. These factors sometimes lead to physical health problems for them.

On the other hand, caregivers also report positive effects from the experience. Taking care of a loved one can bring happiness and a feeling of purpose. One woman who cared for her mother who had Alzheimer's wrote, "I consider that time with her a blessing because I was able to do for her as she did for me, although it wore out both my husband and me to the point of pure physical exhaustion. I would not trade that time of caring for her for anything."[37]

Caregivers who receive help generally cope better with their situation. In some cases, they may be able to arrange for a home health aide to handle daily care, such as bathing and dressing the person with Alzheimer's, and to help with household chores. A visiting nurse may be available to check on the patient and give medications.

It is important for caregivers to take time once in a while to do things they enjoy.

Enrolling the person with Alzheimer's in an adult daycare program can give the caregiver time to handle other necessary matters. These programs give people with Alzheimer's the chance to socialize with others and take part in enjoyable activities, such as crafts or singing. Some offer exercise as part of the program. Since changes in routine can confuse a person with Alzheimer's, they may need time to adjust to a daycare program.

Unfortunately, some people are not able to afford these types of help. Even if this is the case, it is still important for caregivers to take care of themselves, since they cannot provide the best care for their loved one when they are exhausted and ill. Trying to do too much without rest, having unrealistic expectations of how easy Alzheimer's will be to manage, or frustration with the constant lack of control can lead to a state known as caregiver burnout, which is "a state of physical, emotional, and mental exhaustion that may be accompanied by a change in attitude—from positive and caring to negative and unconcerned."[38] Symptoms of caregiver burnout include:

- *Withdrawal from friends and family*
- *Loss of interest in activities previously enjoyed*
- *Feeling blue, irritable, hopeless, and helpless*
- *Changes in appetite, weight, or both*
- *Changes in sleep patterns*
- *Getting sick more often*
- *Feelings of wanting to hurt yourself or the person for whom you are caring*
- *Emotional and physical exhaustion*
- *Excessive use of alcohol and/or sleep medications*
- *Irritability*[39]

Regular self-care is important to prevent caregiver burnout and the negative effects it has on both the caregiver and the patient. Studies show that regular exercise relieves stress, improves sleep, and reduces depression in caregivers. Experts also recommend setting small, easily achievable goals that build toward a larger goal. For example, a caregiver may set a goal to take care of their own health, then start by simply making a doctor's appointment or eating a healthy dinner. Other tips include asking someone else to watch the patient for a few hours so the primary caregiver can take a break, seeing a therapist to talk about negative emotions, taking advantage of support groups that exist for both caregivers and people with Alzheimer's, and learning how to communicate effectively with the person who has Alzheimer's.

Researchers continue to look for ways to help caregivers and people with Alzheimer's cope with their challenges and improve their quality of life. Meanwhile, other researchers are trying to uncover the causes of Alzheimer's in the hope of finding ways to treat or prevent the disease.

## CHAPTER SIX

# MEDICAL ADVANCEMENTS

**M**any important technological advances have been made in the last several decades, and more continue to be made. This improved technology helps people live relatively longer, healthier lives by finding treatments and cures for diseases that past generations never thought possible.

One way researchers are using technology is to study the brain to understand more about the causes of Alzheimer's so it can potentially be prevented. Other researchers are developing new treatments for the symptoms as well as the underlying causes of the disease. Still others are working to find ways of diagnosing Alzheimer's sooner so treatment can have the greatest effect. All of these projects have the potential to positively impact the treatment of Alzheimer's.

## Addressing Risk Factors

Learning about the conditions under which people are more likely to develop Alzheimer's can provide clues for treatment and prevention. An epidemiologic study observes what people do during their everyday lives that may be associated with the development or spread of a disease. Epidemiologic studies are one tool researchers use to examine possible risk factors or preventive measures for Alzheimer's. They try to determine whether there is a link between Alzheimer's and the factor being studied.

Vascular disease, including heart disease, stroke, and diabetes, can decrease blood flow to the brain. Epidemiologic studies have examined whether or not vascular disease increases a person's risk for Alzheimer's. When these studies compared people with and without vascular disease, they found that a higher percentage of people with vascular disease develop Alzheimer's and other cognitive problems.

This raises the question of whether or not controlling the factors that put a person at risk for vascular disease can also decrease a person's risk for developing Alzheimer's. The risk factors for vascular disease include high blood pressure, obesity, high levels of triglycerides (fats in the blood), and insulin resistance. Ongoing studies are testing whether treatments for these conditions may also lower a person's risk for Alzheimer's.

Women are much more likely than men to develop Alzheimer's.

It has been known for years that women are more likely to develop Alzheimer's than men, but for a long time, researchers believed this was because women tend to live longer than men. However, new research into the differences in brain chemistry between women and men have shown that this is not the real reason.

In August 2017, a study found that women who have the genes that are linked to increased Alzheimer's risk have a much greater chance than men of developing the disease between the ages of 65 and 75. With this knowledge, new medical research can take women's brain chemistry into account—for example, they have a higher level of the hormone estrogen than men. Some researchers believe the start of menopause—a period of time when a woman's body changes and her estrogen levels drop—may have something to do with increasing a woman's risk.

## Unproven Treatments

In addition to medications, scientists are investigating the possible effects of certain foods or supplements. These include antioxidants, such as vitamins A and E. Free radical molecules can damage cells. Some researchers believe free radicals play a role in the brain damage patients with Alzheimer's experience. Because antioxidants bind to free radicals and prevent them from damaging cells, researchers believe antioxidants can lower a person's risk for Alzheimer's, and some studies are focusing on using them in new drugs to see if they can also help fight the effects of Alzheimer's after symptoms start.

Unfortunately, some trials have shown that antioxidants will not have the hoped-for effect. One large clinical trial, the Prevention of Alzheimer's Disease by Vitamin E and Selenium (PREADViSE), followed 3,786 older men for 7 years. The results found no difference in the participants' Alzheimer's risk. One explanation the researchers gave for this was that the people who participated in the trial had a lower risk to start with, so it might not have been able to go any lower. Another was that taking vitamin E pills might not have been helpful. According to the Alzheimer's Drug Discovery Foundation,

*Most vitamin E supplements (including those used in the PREADViSE trial) only contain one [form of vitamin E], called alpha-tocopherol. Recent research is revealing that other vitamin E members, such as gamma-tocopherol and beta-tocotrienol, may also be important for health ... multiple observational studies have shown that high dietary intake of vitamin E is linked to a 20–25% lower risk of Alzheimer's disease. Thus, choosing a healthy diet rich in many forms of vitamin E may offer greater benefit for brain health compared to taking supplements.*[40]

There is evidence to suggest that foods high in vitamin E, such as the ones shown here, may help lower the risk of Alzheimer's.

Another supplement under study is ginkgo biloba. Some people take this herb in the hope that it will prevent Alzheimer's. So far, clinical trials have not shown this result. "It just is very solid that it doesn't work as a preventive treatment for Alzheimer's disease,"[41] Oscar Lopez said.

Besides damage from free radicals, some researchers believe inflammation may play a role in the damage Alzheimer's does to the brain. This has led them to investigate the effects that nonsteroidal anti-inflammatory drugs (NSAIDs), such as ibuprofen and naproxen, may have on the prevention of Alzheimer's. Some studies have suggested that taking NSAIDs may reduce a person's risk for Alzheimer's, but clinical trials have not found evidence to support this. In fact, some research has shown that taking NSAIDs later in the disease's progression can do more harm than good because "their anti-inflammatory effects might interfere with the body's self-protective response."[42]

Another theory that has yet to be proven is whether medical marijuana is helpful to people with Alzheimer's. Some experts believe tetrahydrocannabinol (THC), one of the active ingredients in marijuana, can help protect the brain from Alzheimer's. One study published in the *Journal of Alzheimer's Disease* did find that low doses of THC—much lower than what is naturally found in the plant—may be effective in stopping plaques from forming and lowering inflammation. Cannabidiol (CBD), the other active ingredient, is also being studied, and is preferred because it "does not cause the 'high' associated with THC. Research from Barcelona, Spain, published in the *Journal of Alzheimer's Disease* in early 2015, found that a combination of THC and CBD helped prevent degenerative brain symptoms in mice that had been genetically induced to develop Alzheimer's."[43] CBD also produces a relaxed effect, which may help people with Alzheimer's who experience paranoia or restlessness, although some studies have shown no effect on behavioral symptoms. Experts warn that more research is necessary to confirm these findings and that people should not smoke marijuana to try to relieve or prevent Alzheimer's symptoms, especially since the doses researchers are experimenting with are much lower than a person would absorb by smoking marijuana leaves.

Yet another treatment that is currently being researched is an insulin nose spray. Insulin is a hormone that helps regulate blood sugar, and because type 2 diabetes—a disease that makes the body resistant to insulin—is associated with a higher risk of Alzheimer's, scientists already know that a link exists between insulin and Alzheimer's. However, giving someone without diabetes too much insulin can cause problems such as anxiety, confusion, and vision changes. Some studies have shown that when it is sprayed into the nose, insulin reaches the brain quickly and improves memory for people with mild Alzheimer's; however, more research must be done to see whether it will work for most people and what the long-term effects will be.

Many other things have been reported to reduce the risk of Alzheimer's, including extra virgin olive oil, coconut oil, and wine. Although these may help, people should not trust claims that these foods will be 100 percent effective in preventing Alzheimer's or that they will be effective at all in reversing the damage that has already been done by the disease. They should also remember to eat everything, even recommended foods, in moderation. For instance, although one glass of wine per day may help reduce the risk of Alzheimer's, excessive drinking may increase the risk for other diseases, such as breast cancer and liver disease. Additionally, in people younger than 21, any amount of alcohol can have negative effects on the brain because it is still developing.

## Keeping the Brain Active

In addition to physical factors, scientists are studying whether keeping mentally active may affect a person's risk for Alzheimer's. Several studies show a relationship between activities that engage the brain and a lower risk for Alzheimer's. For example, one four-year study compared older people who frequently took part in brain-stimulating activities, such as reading newspapers, doing crossword puzzles, and going to museums, with older people who did such things less frequently. When the investigators compared the number of people in each group who developed Alzheimer's, they found a 47 percent lower risk in the group that frequently did the brain-stimulating activities.

Doing activities that engage the brain may help lower a person's risk of Alzheimer's.

Some studies suggest that people who have more social ties have a decreased risk for cognitive decline. Others show that people with more years of education appeared to have a decreased risk for dementia.

Researchers are trying to figure out the meaning of these results. One explanation is that exercising the brain frequently helps it stay strong, just like a muscle stays strong with physical exercise. According to the Alzheimer's Association, "research has found that keeping the brain active seems to increase its vitality and may build its reserves of brain cells and connections. You could even generate new brain cells."[44]

Another possibility is that factors such as lower mental and social engagement are not a cause of the disease but an effect of it. Some study participants who took part in fewer social and mental activities may have done so because Alzheimer's had already taken hold in their brains. They may have been experiencing the effects of the disease at a stage that was too early to be diagnosed.

In the studies involving education, researchers are also unsure what is responsible for the effect. People who receive more education often also have better financial circumstances and access to better health care. These other factors, rather than the education itself, could be responsible for the results.

## Studying Cause and Effect

Even when evidence shows that a factor is associated with the risk for Alzheimer's, this does not necessarily mean that it causes Alzheimer's or that controlling it will prevent the disease. Martha L. Daviglus, professor of medicine and preventive medicine at Northwestern University, explained, "These associations are examples of the classic chicken or the egg quandary. Are people able to stay mentally sharp over time because they are physically active and socially engaged or are they simply more likely to stay physically active and socially engaged because they are mentally sharp? An association only tells us that these things are related, not that one causes the other."[45] More research is needed to shed light on the relationship between Alzheimer's and possible risk factors.

Although experts cannot say for sure that controlling diet, exercise, or other factors will help prevent Alzheimer's, some of these strategies carry other benefits. For example, exercising and lowering high blood pressure are good for a person's physical health. Social and brain-stimulating activities can help a person enjoy life and are good for mental and emotional health.

## Earlier Detection Methods

Some scientists are researching ways to find out as early as possible whether a person has Alzheimer's. Everyone, even young people, forgets things sometimes, so the early cognitive changes may not always be recognized, even by experts. Some new tests have recently shown promising results, but more research is

# Using Other Medications

Certain types of medications are found to treat more than just the condition they were invented for. Some medications currently being researched for their effects on Alzheimer's include:

- *Blood pressure medication:* A study at Johns Hopkins University found that blood pressure medication may lower Alzheimer's risk by as much as 50 percent, although they are unsure why this is.

- *Diabetes treatments:* A drug called Victoza that helps the body produce insulin has been shown to reduce plaques in the brains of mice by 30 percent within two months and to protect brain cells from further damage. Research is being conducted to see if human brains will react the same way.

- *Rheumatoid arthritis medication:* Rheumatoid arthritis is an autoimmune disease—the body attacks itself, causing inflammation. Researchers hope the medication for this disease, which reduces inflammation, will help protect the brain from Alzheimer's damage. NSAIDs are one type of drug often prescribed for rheumatoid arthritis.

- *Cholesterol medication:* Statins are a type of drug used to treat high cholesterol, and recent research has indicated that high doses of statins may help prevent dementia.

Although researchers are hopeful that at least one of these types of medication may help dementia, much more testing is needed. No one should take any medication they have not been prescribed, and people who have a prescription should follow the directions given by their doctor or pharmacist.

needed to see if these tests will be consistently reliable.

One new test is an eye scan to detect changes in the retina, which is the back of the eye. This scan may show a buildup of Aβ in the retina even before symptoms start appearing. Another test uses peanut butter to detect changes in a person's sense of smell, which is one of the first things to be affected when cognitive decline starts.

Jennifer Stamps, a graduate student at the University of Florida McKnight Brain Institute Center for Smell and Taste, came up with the idea to measure the distance at which a person could smell a spoonful of peanut butter with one nostril.

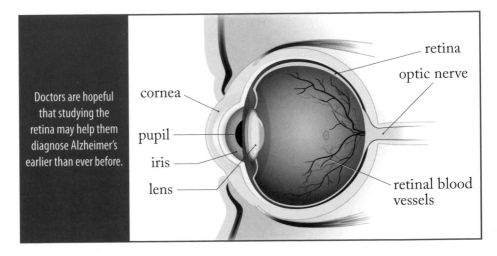

Doctors are hopeful that studying the retina may help them diagnose Alzheimer's earlier than ever before.

retina
optic nerve
cornea
pupil
iris
lens
retinal blood vessels

According to *Medical News Today*,

*The scientists found that patients in the early stages of Alzheimer's disease had a dramatic difference in detecting odor between the left and right nostril—the left nostril was impaired and did not detect the smell until it was an average of 10 cm closer to the nose than the right nostril had made the detection ... This was not the case in patients with other kinds of dementia; instead, these patients had either no differences in odor detection between nostrils or the right nostril was worse at detecting odor than the left one.*[46]

If this test is proven to be accurate, it could be used in clinics that cannot afford expensive scanning equipment. People would even be able to do it at home.

## Changing the Target

Other drugs are being tested to address the other type of Alzheimer's lesion, neurofibrillary tangles, which are made of the protein tau. Tangles form after too many phosphorus molecules bind to tau. Some of the new drugs are designed to prevent this from happening. As with drugs for Aβ, drugs that address tau are often tested on transgenic (genetically modified) mice. These mice have been genetically altered to form tau tangles either alone or along with Aβ plaques.

Some work with transgenic mice suggests that tau causes damage at an earlier stage, before tangles form. If that is the case, treatments that target tangles may act too late, after the damage is already done. Lopez said, "Many investigators are working on disease modifying treatments that can actually get rid of the brain lesions or arrest [stop] the pathological process. But the problem that we're facing is that we don't know what is causing Alzheimer's disease."[47]

Unfortunately, researchers have not had much luck creating a medication to target tau. In July 2016, *TIME* magazine reported that the latest trial of a tau drug had disappointing results: Participants who took the experimental drug showed no changes in their cognitive ability or ability to do daily tasks. However, those who took only the anti-tau drug and no other Alzheimer's medications showed a 33 percent slower rate of brain shrinkage, which indicates that researchers are on the right track and may be able to eventually come up with an anti-tau medication that works.

## Testing a Vaccine for Alzheimer's

Some new drugs being tested target Aβ to stop it from forming or clumping together into plaques. Other drugs under study are designed to remove Aβ from the brain. Scientists are also examining the question of whether the plaques or the oligomers cause the damage.

The transgenic mice used to test this medication have genes implanted that trigger their brains to produce large amounts of Aβ. As a result, the mice's brains develop Alzheimer's-like plaques. One approach first tested on transgenic mice was active immunization against Aβ.

An example of active immunization is the chicken pox vaccine. A doctor injects a child with a weakened form of the chicken pox virus. This triggers the child's immune system to produce antibodies to fight that virus. Similarly, when researchers injected transgenic mice with a vaccine containing Aβ, the mice's immune systems produced antibodies to fight Aβ. As a result of the action of these antibodies, the number of plaques in the mice's brains decreased.

Researchers hoped the vaccine would have the same effect in humans. A clinical trial began but had to be stopped in 2002 because 15 of the 360 participants developed severe brain inflammation. Their immune systems had responded to the vaccine by producing not only antibodies but also other cells that caused the inflammation.

To get around this problem, researchers developed a different approach. This time they tried passive immunization. Instead of triggering the immune system to produce antibodies, passive immunization involves injecting already existing antibodies directly into patients. Klunk explained, "Passive immunization would be equivalent to what a breast-feeding infant gets from its mother, when it gets antibodies in the milk. You just get the antibodies; you don't stimulate the immune system."[48]

Researchers found that one vaccine had the effect of targeting both tau and Aβ, which was a hopeful sign. In July 2016, *Medical News Today* reported that if the vaccine did well in preclinical trials, it could start to be tested on humans within the next three to five years. Another vaccine targets only tau and, as of 2017, had started to be tested on humans. It was still in Phase I, so researchers will need to study participants to make sure the vaccine is effective and safe.

## Studying the Brain

To determine whether new treatments are working and how early they must begin, researchers need to see what happens inside the brains of patients. "The only way to study amyloid in the past was after a person died, and you could open the brain and see the amyloid,"[49] Lopez noted. One drawback of an autopsy is that it shows the damage only at one point in time but does not reveal how the damage progressed. New brain imaging techniques are helping researchers solve this problem.

One technique involves a radioactive tracer known as Pittsburgh compound B (PiB). After being injected into a patient, this tracer binds to Aβ in the patient's brain. The brain is then scanned using positron emission tomography, or a PET scan, which detects the radioactive tracer and creates a picture on a computer screen. PiB shows up in the picture to tell researchers where plaques exist. Klunk, who helped invent the compound, stated, "It's allowed us for the first time to be able to see the plaque, the pathology, in a living person."[50] Other similar compounds have also been developed. In 2012, the FDA approved a tracer called florbetapir F18 (known by the brand name Amyvid); in 2013, it approved one called flutemetamol F18 (Vizamyl); and in 2014, it approved one called florbetaben F18 (Neuraceq). These all work the same way PiB does.

This test alone cannot diagnose Alzheimer's, since many people who do not have the

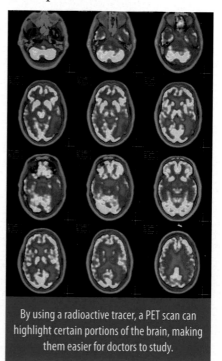

By using a radioactive tracer, a PET scan can highlight certain portions of the brain, making them easier for doctors to study.

disease still have plaques in their brain, but it can help alert doctors to the possibility that their patient might soon develop Alzheimer's. Additionally, it may help researchers see how the brain changes as the disease progresses. Other types of tracers are being developed to detect tau.

Other types of technology can help researchers study the brain as well. In September 2017, an international team of scientists made a major breakthrough in studying tau when they used cryo-electron microscopy (cryo-EM) to look at tau filaments taken from a patient with Alzheimer's during an autopsy. Cryo-EM involves using frozen specimens—in this case, sections of brain matter—under a microscope. Freezing the brain samples makes them easier to see without adding dyes or other chemicals. When the researchers looked at tau proteins, they saw how they were made up:

> *The atomic-level look at tau revealed stacks of concentric double "C" shapes, with a "capital C" shape surrounding a second, "lowercase" c shape reversing itself and curling tightly back inside the first curve. These stacks of multiple copies of amyloid tau filaments run parallel, like finely woven fabric.*

> *The closer look at tau gives insight into why it has proven difficult for scientists to target with potential therapeutics: the tight configuration keeps out water molecules, creating what is known as a "steric zipper." This formation makes the filaments more stable, which in turn makes it more difficult for the cells' natural clearing functions to remove.*[51]

## Using Other Methods

Measuring Aβ with PET scans is only one method being tested to help scientists learn about Alzheimer's progression. PET scans can also show the way the brain uses glucose, a sugar that provides brain cells with energy. A form of glucose with radioactive molecules is injected into a patient, and the PET scan detects it. In patients with Alzheimer's, certain brain areas show decreased glucose metabolism in these scans. Another type of imaging study, magnetic resonance imaging (MRI), uses a magnetic field and sound waves to create a computerized image. Some studies are using MRI to track the way brain areas shrink over time in patients with Alzheimer's.

## The Drug Trial Process

Medications go through an intense trial, or testing, process to make sure they are safe and effective before they are sold. This process has multiple steps. First, preclinical studies are done. In a preclinical study, an experimental drug is examined in test tubes and animals before being tested on humans.

After preclinical trials are done, clinical trials can begin. These have up to four phases:

Phase I: A small study, generally involving fewer than 100 volunteers, that examines the safety of the treatment.

Phase II: A larger study, involving up to several hundred volunteers, that gathers more information about safety, side effects, and dosage. It may offer some indications as to whether the treatment is effective, but the number of participants is too small to provide convincing evidence.

Phase III: Large studies, involving several hundred or several thousand volunteers, that gather evidence about the treatment's effectiveness and whether the benefits outweigh the risks from side effects. The FDA will examine this evidence when deciding whether or not to approve the drug.

After a drug is approved by the FDA, Phase IV trials gather information about long-term effects. Not every drug goes through Phase IV.

Cerebrospinal fluid (CSF), a liquid that surrounds the brain and spinal cord, is also providing clues about

Alzheimer's. Doctors use a small needle to withdraw a CSF sample from a patient's lower back. The sample contains brain chemicals, including the Aβ and tau proteins involved with Alzheimer's. Measuring the amounts of these proteins in CSF may someday allow doctors to diagnose Alzheimer's at an early stage, perhaps before outward symptoms appear. It could also help track the effects of new medications. The Alzheimer's Association has worked to create a standardized procedure that all medical facilities would use when testing CSF. Following this procedure, which is called the Alzheimer's Association QC Program for CSF Biomarkers, ensures that medical facilities get the correct results when they test CSF. They can test their samples for accuracy by comparing their results with the results of other laboratories in the United States and Europe.

## Looking to the Future

The fight against Alzheimer's is ongoing, and there are many participants, including people who have been diagnosed and their friends and family. Since 1989, the Alzheimer's Association has held the Walk to End Alzheimer's, an event to raise both awareness and funds for research. As of 2017, it is held in more than 600 communities across the United States and is the world's largest Alzheimer's event. In 2015, participants raised more than $75 million.

Raising awareness is almost as important as raising funding for medical research. Any medical advancements discovered now will not be available as treatments for several years, and until then, people are living and dying with the disease. Decreasing the stigma and helping a person with Alzheimer's live their life to the fullest will have a positive impact on the patients and loved ones who are directly affected by this disease.

## Introduction:
## Understanding Alzheimer's

1. John Pohlod, interview by Jacqueline Adams, September 27, 2010.

## Chapter One:
## More Than Forgetfulness

2. Quoted in Barry Petersen, "Jan's Story: Love and Early-Onset Alzheimer's," CBS News, June 20, 2010. www.cbsnews.com/stories/2010/06/20/sunday/main6600364.shtml.

3. Quoted in N.C. Berchtold and C.W. Cotman, "Evolution in the Conceptualization of Dementia and Alzheimer's Disease: Greco-Roman Period to the 1960s," *Neurobiology of Aging*, vol. 19, no. 3, 1998, p. 174.

4. Quoted in Berchtold and Cotman, "Evolution in the Conceptualization of Dementia and Alzheimer's Disease: Greco-Roman Period to the 1960s," p. 174.

5. Quoted in Berchtold and Cotman, "Evolution in the Conceptualization of Dementia and Alzheimer's Disease: Greco-Roman Period to the 1960s," pp. 174–175.

6. Quoted in Nawab Qizilbash et al., eds., *Evidence-Based Dementia Practice*. Oxford, UK: Blackwell Science, 2002, p. 209.

7. Quoted in Peter J. Whitehouse, Konrad Maurer, and Jesse F. Ballenger, *Concepts of Alzheimer Disease: Biological, Clinical, and Cultural*

*Perspectives.* Baltimore, MD: The Johns Hopkins University Press, 2000, e-book.

8. Quoted in Whitehouse, Maurer, and Ballenger, *Concepts of Alzheimer Disease.*

9. Quoted in Berchtold and Cotman, "Evolution in the Conceptualization of Dementia and Alzheimer's Disease: Greco-Roman Period to the 1960s," p. 180.

10. Robert Katzman, "The Prevalence and Malignancy of Alzheimer's Disease: A Major Killer," *Archives of Neurology,* April 1976, p. 217.

11. Quoted in "History of Alzheimer's Disease," Kalamazoo Center for Medical Studies, 2005–2006. hod.kcms.msu.edu/timeline.php?y=1901-1906.

12. François Boller and Margaret M. Forbes, "History of Dementia and Dementia in History: An Overview," *Journal of the Neurological Sciences,* vol. 158, 1998, p. 131.

## Chapter Two:
## Alzheimer's and Other Dementias

13. Oscar Lopez, interview by Jacqueline Adams, May 20, 2010.

14. "Dementia with Lewy Bodies," Alzheimer's Association, accessed August 31, 2017. www.alz.org/dementia/dementia-with-lewy-bodies-symptoms.asp.

15. William Klunk, interview by Jacqueline Adams, May 17, 2010.

16. Klunk, interview.

17. Lopez, interview.

18. "Mild Cognitive Impairment," Alzheimer's Association, accessed August 31, 2017. www.alz.org/dementia/mild-cognitive-impairment-mci.asp.

19. Angela Lunde, "Myths, Misconceptions Interfere with Alzheimer's Diagnosis, Care," Mayo Clinic, June 26, 2012. www.mayoclinic.org/diseases-conditions/alzheimers-disease/expert-blog/alzheimers-stigma/bgp-20055844.

## Chapter Three:
## The Science Behind Alzheimer's

20. Robin Brisbourne, "Why Do Some People Get Dementia and Not Others?," Alzheimer's Research UK Blog, July 21, 2015. www.dementia-blog.org/why-do-some-people-get-dementia/.

21. Ronald Petersen, MD, "Rapidly Progressing Alzheimer's: Something Else?," Mayo Clinic, October 22, 2014. www.mayoclinic.org/diseases-conditions/alzheimers-disease/expert-answers/alzheimers/faq-20058510.

## Chapter Four:
## Treatment for Alzheimer's

22. Klunk, interview.

23. Klunk, interview.

24. Lopez, interview.

25. Quoted in Milt Freudenheim, "Many Alzheimer's Patients Find Comfort in Books," *New York Times*, April 22, 2010. newoldage.blogs.nytimes.com/2010/04/22/many-alzheimers-patients-find-comfort-in-books/.

## Chapter Five:
## Making Adjustments

26. Quoted in R. Morgan Griffin, "What It's Like to Have Dementia," WebMD, 2009. www.webmd.com/brain/features/understanding-dementia-symptoms?page=3.

27. Kathy Hatfield, "What a Spread!," *KnowItAlz*, March 25, 2010. www.knowitalz.com/community/alzheimer-s/what-a-spread.html.

28. *Caring for a Person with Alzheimer's Disease*, National Institute on Aging, National Institutes of Health, March 2010, p. 12.

29. "When People with Dementia Refuse Help," Social Care Institute for Excellence, May 2015. www.scie.org.uk/dementia/living-with-dementia/difficult-situations/refusing-help.asp.

30. Stephen Soreff, "Understanding and Dealing with Resident Aggression: Exploring the Extent, Causes, and Impact of Aggressive Outbursts and How to Handle Them," *Nursing Homes*, March 2004. findarticles.com/p/articles/mi_m3830/is_3_53/ai_n6066074/.

31. Quoted in Deborah Franklin, "Camp for Alzheimer's Patients Isn't About Memories," National Public Radio, September 6, 2010. www.npr.org/templates/story/story.php?storyId=129607201&ft=1&f=3.

32. "When a Person with Alzheimer's Rummages and Hides Things," National Institute on Aging, July 23, 2017. www.nia.nih.gov/health/when-person-alzheimers-rummages-and-hides-things.

33. Quoted in "Understanding Hallucinations and Delusions in Alzheimer's," Alzheimers.net, May 6, 2014. www.alzheimers.net/2014-05-06/hallucinations-and-delusions/.

34. Quoted in Dennis Thompson Jr., "Dealing with Hallucinations and Delusions in Alzheimer's," Everyday Health, December 29, 2008. www.everydayhealth.com/alzheimers/alzheimers-hallucinations-and-delusions.aspx.

35. Quoted in Griffin, "What It's Like to Have Dementia."

36. Quoted in Elizabeth Landau, "Children of Alzheimer's Sufferers Want to Know Their Risk," CNN, July 20, 2010. www.cnn.com/2010/HEALTH/07/16/alzheimer.guidelines/index.html.

37. "Barbara's Story," Alzheimer's Association, September 8, 2008. www.alz.org/living_with_alzheimers_14446.asp.

38. "Recognizing Caregiver Burnout," WebMD, May 10, 2017. www.webmd.com/women/caregiver-recognizing-burnout#1.

39. "Recognizing Caregiver Burnout," WebMD.

# Chapter Six:
# Medical Advancements

40. Yuko Hara, "Antioxidant Supplements Fail to Prevent Dementia in Older Men," Alzheimer's Drug Discovery Foundation, April 10, 2017. www.alzdiscovery.org/cognitive-vitality/blog/antioxidant-supplements-fail-to-prevent-dementia-in-older-men.

41. Lopez, interview.

42. James M. Ellison, "A New Angle on Alzheimer's Disease: The Inflammation Connection," BrightFocus Foundation, January 3, 2017. www.brightfocus.org/alzheimers/article/new-angle-alzheimers-disease-inflammation-connection.

43. Melanie Haiken, "Medical Marijuana and Alzheimer's," Caring.com, May 16, 2017. www.caring.com/articles/medical-marijuana-alzheimers-effects.

44. "Stay Mentally Active," Alzheimer's Association, accessed September 7, 2017. www.alz.org/we_can_help_stay_mentally_active.asp.

45. Quoted in "Independent Panel Finds Insufficient Evidence to Support Preventive Measures for Alzheimer's Disease," National Institutes of Health, April 28, 2010. www.nih.gov/news/health/apr2010/od-28.htm.

46. Belinda Weber, "Peanut Butter Could Help Diagnose Alzheimer's Disease," *Medical News Today*, July 8, 2015. www.medicalnewstoday.com/articles/267236.php.

47. Lopez, interview.

48. Klunk, interview.

49. Lopez, interview.

50. Klunk, interview.

51. "First-Ever Atomic Look at Tau Fibril Structure in Alzheimer's Reveals Detailed Pathways," National Institute on Aging, September 6, 2017. www.nia.nih.gov/news/first-ever-atomic-look-tau-fibril-structure-alzheimers-reveals-detailed-pathways.

**acetylcholine:** A neurotransmitter that helps the brain form memories.

**acetylcholinesterase:** An enzyme that breaks down acetylcholine.

**amyloid beta (Aβ):** Small protein pieces that clump together to form plaques in the brains of people with Alzheimer's.

**amyloid plaque:** An abnormal clump of Aβ protein that builds up between neurons in people with Alzheimer's disease.

**atrophy:** Shrinkage.

**axon:** Part of a neuron through which chemical messengers and other materials are transported.

**cerebrospinal fluid (CSF):** A liquid that surrounds the brain and spinal cord.

**cholinesterase inhibitor:** A drug that stops or slows down acetylcholinesterase in order to prevent it from interfering with communication between neurons.

**chromosomes:** Strings of genes that are coiled up into packages inside cells.

**clinical trial:** A study that takes place under controlled conditions.

**computerized tomography (CT)/computerized axial tomography (CAT):** A type of imaging study that puts together X-rays from many different angles to form a cross-sectional image.

**dementia:** A condition in which the brain's ability to function is impaired to the point that it interferes with daily life.

**dendrite:** A thin branch of a neuron that receives chemical messages.

**enzyme:** A protein that speeds up or enables a specific chemical reaction.

**epidemiologic study:** A study of disease patterns based on observations of factors in people's everyday lives.

**free radicals:** Oxygen and nitrogen molecules that combine readily with other molecules.

**geriatrician:** A doctor who specializes in the health care and diseases of the elderly.

**glutamate:** A neurotransmitter involved with memory.

**hippocampus:** A brain area involved with learning and converting short-term memories into long-term memories.

**inflammation:** An immune system reaction to infection or injury.

**lesion:** An abnormal change in tissue.

**magnetic resonance imaging (MRI):** A type of imaging study that uses a magnetic field and sound waves to create a computerized image.

**memantine:** A drug that protects neurons by preventing too much glutamate from entering neuron receptors.

**mild cognitive impairment (MCI):** A condition in which people have greater memory problems than are normal for their age but not as severe as the memory problems of people with dementia.

**neurodegenerative:** Causing brain tissue to deteriorate over time.

**neurofibrillary tangle:** A lesion made of abnormal, twisted threads of tau protein that forms inside neurons in people with Alzheimer's disease.

**neuron:** A nerve cell.

**neuropsychological testing:** Tests of different cognitive abilities, including memory, language, and problem solving.

**neurotransmitter:** Chemical messenger that delivers signals from one neuron to another.

**oligomer:** A small accumulation of up to a dozen Aβ sections stuck together.

**positron emission tomography (PET):** A type of imaging study that detects radiation inside the body and translates it into a computerized image.

**sundowning:** Increased agitation in the late afternoon or evening.

**synapse:** The gap between neurons.

**tau:** A protein that binds to a neuron's transport tubes to keep them stable.

**Alzheimer's Association**
225 N. Michigan Ave., Fl. 17
Chicago, IL 60601
toll-free 24/7 helpline: (800) 272-3900
info@alz.org
alz.org
This global organization provides funding for research and support as well as educational materials to those affected by Alzheimer's disease. Its website contains detailed information about the disease and ways to live with it, downloadable publications, and other resources for patients and caregivers.

**Alzheimer's Disease Education and Referral (ADEAR) Center**
(800) 438-4380
adear@nia.nih.gov
www.nia.nih.gov/health/alzheimers
The center is operated by the National Institute on Aging as a comprehensive source of information about Alzheimer's disease. Its information specialists answer questions, provide publications, and refer people to other sources if necessary. Publications can also be downloaded from the website.

**Alzheimer's Disease International (ADI)**
64 Great Suffolk St.
London SE1 0BL
United Kingdom
info@alz.co.uk
www.alz.co.uk
This organization works to establish and strengthen Alzheimer's organizations around the world and to raise awareness about Alzheimer's disease and other dementias. Its website contains information about the disease, help for people who have it and for their caregivers, and downloadable publications.

**National Institute on Aging (NIA)**
Building 31, Rm. 5C27
31 Center Dr., MSC 2292
Bethesda, MD 20892
(800) 222-2225
www.nia.nih.gov
One of the National Institutes of Health, this agency
supports and conducts research related to aging, trains
scientists, and provides information. It leads the federal
effort on Alzheimer's disease research. Its website
includes many downloadable publications and
information on numerous studies.

# FOR MORE INFORMATION

## Books

Atkins, Charles. *The Alzheimer's Answer Book: Professional Answers to More than 250 Questions About Alzheimer's and Dementia.* Naperville, IL: Sourcebooks, 2008.
Atkins provides easy-to-understand answers to questions about many aspects of Alzheimer's disease, including causes, prevention, diagnosis, treatment, and caregiving.

Brackey, Jolene. *Creating Moments of Joy Along the Alzheimer's Journey.* West Lafayette, IN: Purdue University Press, 2017.
This book helps soften the blow of Alzheimer's for both the patient and their caregivers.

Mace, Nancy L., and Peter V. Rabins. *The 36-Hour Day: A Family Guide to Caring for People Who Have Alzheimer Disease, Other Dementias, and Memory Loss.* 6th ed. Baltimore, MD: Johns Hopkins University Press, 2017.
This valuable guide written to help families cope with Alzheimer's disease includes many real-life examples.

Scott, Paula Spencer. *Surviving Alzheimer's: Practical Tips and Soul-Saving Wisdom for Caregivers.* San Francisco, CA: Eva-Birch Media, 2014.
This book gives caregivers helpful advice on how to help a loved one with Alzheimer's without putting too much stress on themselves.

Snyder, Lisa. *Speaking Our Minds: What It's Like to Have Alzheimer's.* Baltimore, MD: Health Professions Press, 2009.
Through interviews with seven diverse people, Snyder helps caregivers understand what is going on in the minds of their loved ones.

## Websites

**The Alzheimer's Research Forum**
www.alzforum.org
This scientific community provides the latest news, research databases, discussion forums, and interviews about the disease.

**AlzOnline**
alzonline.phhp.ufl.edu
This website gives important tips for caregivers, including stress management, self-care, planning for the future, and how to find services that can provide additional help.

**Brain Basics: Know Your Brain**
www.ninds.nih.gov/Disorders/Patient-Caregiver-Education/Know-Your-Brain
This website, created by the National Institute of Neurological Disorders and Stroke, gives an in-depth look at how a healthy brain functions and the ways neurological disorders such as Alzheimer's disrupt it.

**HBO: The Alzheimer's Project**
www.hbo.com/alzheimers
This website features a four-part documentary and fifteen short films about many aspects of Alzheimer's.

**Mayo Clinic**
www.mayoclinic.org/diseases-conditions/alzheimers-disease/home/ovc-20167098
The Alzheimer's section of this world-renowned medical center's website contains detailed information about the disease, multimedia resources, answers to questions, and an expert blog.

## A

## B

# ABOUT THE AUTHOR

**Jennifer Lombardo** earned her BA in English from the University at Buffalo and still resides in Buffalo, New York. She has helped write a number of books for young adults on topics ranging from world history to body image. In her spare time, she enjoys cross-stitching, hiking, and volunteering with local organizations.